I, FAUST

Copyright © 1986-2007 by Matthew Hong

All rights reserved.

Library of Congress Cataloging-in-Publication Data
Hong, Matthew.
I, Faust / Matthew Hong.
LCCN 2006910272

Published by Aria Press, New York

Hardcover : ISBN 13 : 978-0-9791184-0-1 / ISBN 10 : 0-9791184-0-9
Paperback : ISBN 13 : 978-0-9791184-1-8 / ISBN 10 : 0-9791184-1-7

Portions of the text have appeared in the following publications and productions: The American Aesthetic Journal, Arcade Magazine, The Artists' Quarter, *The Beat Generation*, COMPAS, Cacophony Chorus, Coffee House Poets, Colors Magazine, L'Ecole Meyerhold, Fresh Air Radio, KFAI, Kuppernicus, The Loft, *no place (like home)*, Pixel Press, Poets Want to Sing, Saint Paul Art Crawl, Sparrow, Spoken/Unspoken, SpeakOut, SPAC, SPNN, Walker Art Center, Write on Radio.

www.ifaust.com | info@ifaust.com

For information on rights, permissions, and distribution, please contact:

Aria Press
www.ariapress.com | info@ariapress.com
1-646-216-9669

Matthew Hong

CONTENTS

AUTHOR'S PREFACE / 7

DEDICATION / 13

PRELUDE / 17

THE FIRST QUARTER / 25

THE SECOND QUARTER / 87

INTERLUDE / 155

THE THIRD QUARTER / 169

THE FOURTH QUARTER / 273

POSTLUDE / 323

APPENDIX : CITIES & DUST / 333

AUTHOR'S PREFACE

"Whereof one cannot speak, thereof one must remain silent."
Wittgenstein reminds us of the tautology. The opposite holds
equally true. Historical Necessity. There is also Poetic Necessity.

The following selection is an epic poem. *I, Faust,* now after some
twenty years in the making, still, in many ways, I concede, seems
scarcely the beginning. And as such, you will be forgiving
in your reading.

The epic poem is a form that is lost. It is a form that is difficult
to take on, much more difficult to complete, and recognition,
if any, almost always irreverent. Northrop Frye says, "The epic
is not a poem by a poet, but that poet's poem," adding that
it is not possible to have more than one, with the exception
of course of Homer, who had two. It took Goethe sixty years
for *his* Faust. Perhaps I still have a long way to go. I believe
Zeno had something to say about this.

Having spent the better half of my life towards this work, one might suppose that its reason for being would be self-evident, as in the form which has evolved. This, however, remains to become so. I have had many *demons* to struggle, as it were, questioning my endurance and the sheer feasibility of this undertaking. One could premise a book solely on the virtues of this attempt. I shall not be the one to do it. I still have many things I would like to add or take away from the current text. There is a lesson to be learned in letting go. In the end, it may be that the poem simply *is*.

Contained in this edition is the appendix. It is a selection of letters and abstracts of reflections gathered over the same twenty year period as the working of *I, Faust*. What can I say? Pure indulgence. Certainly I could not call upon that same pretext of Poetic Necessity. Here I shall plead, necessity of the social type. One easily acknowledges the occurrence of such musings on the peculiar part of the poet. To explain the act of binding it with the manuscript proper would require further investigation. An argument that the appendix aspires to be a literary piece unto itself can be fashioned. Indeed, it carries its own title, *Cities & Dust*. This argument, presumably, for it to be worthy in the final count, must be conceived within the text itself. For now, we might make an allowance for this epistolary post-script of sorts in the present state for its sheer eagerness to further substantiate this edition, even if only with respect to volume. And, though one might deduce that the letters were excavated of certain extraordinary moments, here I shall forewarn that too often these entries are equal to the banal. The reader would show compassion in taking them to be witness to that existence which was to become a fact for the author in the writing of this poem. Whatever it be, like a certain phenomenon, I can only speak of its effect – its cause remaining veiled. Considering the text of the poem and the appendix together, one perceives sufficient intimation of the other in the regard of each. Without deferring to call them two halves of whatever whole, one sees a kind of reciprocity between the two entities beginning to emerge. If one is the interior, the other, exterior, and vice versa. One is the manifestation while the other is the socio-historical climate which precipitates it. The two inform each other in the sharing of their semblable event history, or genealogy – their independent evolutions having procured parallel paths.

This recalls other incidences of this literary event often posthumous and of much more merit than that of my own present attempt. Kafka, Crane, Stevens, et al. The integrity of this device is generally born of the passing away of the author, then championed by the respective trustee towards the greater understanding of the artist's work. It would then follow that with the case at hand, the integrity of the work and the life of its author are mutually exclusive. Granted. I shall not presently involve this dichotomy. The evolution of this piece would perhaps later arrive at its own justification.

I should be wise in forthcoming with the necessary preemptive measures, such as those disclaiming any resemblances to real people, real lives, etc. – this thing composed primarily of moments which were funded in importance more in the metaphysical realm than anywhere else. But alas, in the end, I will admit that it resembles all too well a certain reality undeniable. Nonetheless, I have stricken all proper names of people and replaced them with those of cities, eradicating all allusions to anything delicate other than my own emotional and spiritual state. As such, any libelous tendency is targeted at myself and falls under the auspices of a poet's prerogative of self-deprecation, the perennial clause which grants us such license.

Concerning the condition of this manuscript entire, I am once more without pretext. Atrocities may abound. And, the lack of structural soundness of an abstracted work-in-progress, or, the more important half of *this* tautology, a work *not-yet-complete*, is all too present, resulting in these parts which feign not to predicate a whole. The ostensible inconsistencies are a natural consequence. In short, this is a curious presentation, the intent of which I am not prepared to defend. Enough. Justice, then, is served, not to the written word in the current outing of this manuscript, but to those people without whose support I could not have made it thus far.

Therefore, to no occasion, I have published this text for the pleasure (or pain) of a few friends.

– MH / 2007

DEDICATION

There is no listening
to the western winds.

There are no secrets
in the greenery.

These statues see not
the passing of time.

The birds sing to them
but they hear no song,

With brushes witless,
if not dumb to tell.

I have journeyed to
this garden again

To look into the
dark reliquary,

And to see the leaves
trapped in the fountains

Dissolving blood-like
into marble lines.

With fallen faces
of angels cast out,

The viewer passes
not their troubled eyes,

Their breath of fire hushed
over centuries.

Should they speak, their braised
tongues lock in stone jaws.

They stand poised with their
mouths pursed and waiting

For that slight reprieve
that they might achieve,

Once more, the air of
the mist of morning.

PRELUDE

[I]

i.

All things stood still, it
seemed. Even the stars

Abstained their dancing
on the frozen lakes.

The water, being
stern in solitude,

Would not ripple nor
shimmer in the dark.

Four and twenty years
but what has happened?

Nothing by way of
what can last. And now,

Partitioned in this
pedantry of lies,

In latter days of
an ill-destined life

I retrace the ways
through the seasons past.

ii.

Perhaps it was here,
the untold story,

A plot forgotten
of antiquity.

Centuries of heat
and incandescence

Stirring the vision,
and the primal wind

Moving fast over
the face of this land

Shaping the sand to
the wisdom of dunes.

How many moons waxed
by the sparrow's wings?

–Their last fluttered dance
against the first frost.

How many rising
tides widened to rest?

Their slow encroachment
had been heard at night.

Perhaps a people
conceived to build here.

Perhaps in waking
they prayed for the rain.

iii.

How many nights spent
beholding the earth

And the sky as one,
waiting, wanting. But

Then to wonder at
the demarcation

Brought by dawn, still
to wonder at the light

From which I turn my
eyes and only feel

The transformation:
the heat of the sun,

The passion; the chill
of marble and stone.

Attending the night
sober without sleep

I pace by open
windows to observe

The curtains dancing,
within them shifting

Of the wind, of the
things unseen, charged high

By some spectral past
of ways forgotten,

The faint chimeras
imploring as if

Of lovers sweating
with wanton fever

In voluptuousness
swollen with intent.

iv.

Darkness will recoil
its splintering hands.

This night is captive
to the slated course.

My domain without
borders, my sole realm

Void of substance, I
concede to the dawn

And I am left half
wanting, half afraid.

Shall I try this time
to hold the waning?

It does not last, this
night, it will pass on,

As all things in turn
will submit themselves.

Innocence, fragile
and trembling of fear,

Soon awakened, its
repose soon upset;

The silencing touch
of a lover's hand,

Soon withered and grown
cold, soon forgotten;

The cool wind and the
fluttering of leaves

Soon turned to ice, so
soon cast to their deaths.

What whim, what detail
of spring can endure?

Tired, tired and afraid,
very much afraid,

The head lays itself
to rest without ease.

THE FIRST QUARTER

[II]

i.

These wayward paths had
come covered with snow.

So quickly the leaves,
their colors expired,

Had seen their yearly
end, one after one

To the very last.
Tonight for a time

Quiescent is the
wind, full of repose.

ii.

You trace the crusted
course which leads you back

In time to that spring
you failed to attend.

In memories that
search through fallen years,

Shoes release the prints
of recollection

And lose footing in
the retrieving past.

iii.

When you arrive you
will knock at the door

Hinging on fragile
reminiscence. And

Nostalgia will in
empty halls resound,

You anticipate–
Soon enough. For now

A long way from where
you are, further still,

Made longer by the
night, the snow, the chill.

Meanwhile you walk the
path which leads you back

In time to that spring
you stray to retrieve.

iv.

You will inquire the
lamp post on the way

Of brownstone mansions
and of histories.

So many times you
walked these nights before

Never questioning
to where they would lead.

A cracked stone recessed
in the crumbling wall,

The old bicycle
fastened to the fence

Still there, slowly with
it becoming one.

These are the etchings
of the elements,

Frozen incidents
which recall to you

The proper way home.
You are almost there.

[III]

i.

Contained in the wake
was the restless wind,

Cognate concessions
in the fields of rape

Of what the primal
lexicon ensured.

You saw the shadow
flanked in the landscape

And came to realize
the first flight of birds.

The soil in silence
you cultivated,

Your hidden garden
you tended, assured

Nothing stood between
earth and the heavens

With myths of fire and
salt, bread unleavened.

ii.

Greater than any
of Solomon's psalms,

The contradiction
in the stolen seeds

Whose fragile words you
held in open palms,

Fermented with heat,
you would watch them bleed.

You sat and wrote by
the strict rows of corn

And in the page you
traced the cries of crows

So by this rite the
passage would be sworn.

To this distance you
drove with intent, your

God beyond belief,
blackened and faceless,

The ladder climbed of
Jacob's discontent,

The angel fallen
with little reprieve.

iii.

The tangled thread of
knowledge that you searched,

The books that perched high
in gilded cages

Waiting to be freed
by an unclaimed mind,

The unread pages
of an afterthought,

The lines in rhymed and
metered verses wrought.

The procession of
wearied foot soldiers

In trenches dug of
boyish hands wagered

In the recesses
of a diary

Where sand sculptures at
their dusk were leveled

By encroaching tides,
and small stones beveled

By waters remained
innocent, unseen.

[IV]

i.

Insist upon the
night this much—our lives

In perpetual
conflict, and factions

Divided in the
common core, our cries

Unforgiven in
the mitigation,

And certainties made
uncertain in deeds,

Complicit without
will, without motion,

Our own wavering
in the wind like reeds,

May one day become
steadfast in action.

There is much of what
we have not yet lived.

The correlative
of this objective

Emotion, feigning,
has been unfounded,

Elusive as this
ill disposition.

ii.

Insist upon the
night this much—our eyes

That see no further
than what is, this tide,

And hopes shattered in
triangulations,

Our dreams dismembered
in our wild wakings,

With melancholia
obscure and extreme

In how we die to
live a dying life,

May strive beyond such
years to simply be.

iii.

This was not the plan.
The fantastical

Force of this nature
descends. And like the

Directionless breeze–
What does it matter?

One cannot speak; no
doubt one is silent.

It follows of need.
What will need follow?

Nothing relative
to wage the progress,

Only telling, these
hands, cracked and flaking,

Forming twin tablets
of an open book

With lines that draw the
difficult story.

Would I remember
the ancestral code?

Where, harbinger of
chaos and defeat?

iv.

Insist upon the
night this much–our fears

Against which with all
our strength we contend

And still be broken
to this slated end,

Being fully in
our constitution

To engage in peace
yet one more struggle,

May find hate and in
union be disposed.

v.

What matters now, these
demands, first waxen,

But then laid to rest
in expiration?

The savage son will
advocate the pain.

Insist upon the
night to remember

The fault of aged men
who stare witlessly

Upon the pages
of their history.

Our charge of primal
insignificance

Have made principles
of our not knowing.

vi.

The discord begins.
One by one they are

Maligned, and in them
you have taken course.

Never to know the
next move or station,

You cannot live out
this predicament.

What power vested
creating order

By day by the same
force creates by night

A new disorder.
I know of one who

*Sought the exactest
of expressions in*

*The deadest of nights
in the deepest core*

Of his hurried heart.
Imminence of the

Foreboding shimmers
like an obsession

Tapered to a blade.
The pathology

In the loss of self
sees the counterfeit.

You have played out the
worst of circumstance.

You have created
an essence of this.

It ends with you not
knowing your own face.

vii.

Insist upon the
night this much—our cries

Transposed in time, stripped
in the azure seam,

Vanishing deftly
like the breath of God

Will ascend somewhere
and be heard at last.

All of happiness,
fleeting and worthless.

Modes of time and space
—would it be this place?

It might be this night.
Sages full of rage,

Expound in verse to
make the concession,

Where but to speak is
to end the sorrow.

We have longed for it,
this much longed for thing.

Render to ease the
evening's dissension.

[V]

i.

There are some men the
rain cannot weather.

They stand in outer
rings of circumstance

With paper cups and
unlit cigarettes.

They wait by the news-
stands under awnings

Inhabiting pools
of slow reaction

Watching for something
sudden to occur.

—*Blue is the taste of
April's opium.*

ii.

Again eternal
in endless cycles

The soil again turns
released from the frost

And the greenery
grows despite itself

For another year.
—April is irony.

Every season will
have its metaphors;

Every month its own
catalogue of words;

Each moment its swift
inflection passing.

*...But mostly, April
becomes twice removed.*

iii.

Indeed. What we are
and what we are not

In contemplation
idly contemplate.

Reflexively in
thoughts we think ourselves

As less than complete,
pacing vacant lots,

Questioning blossoms
and the rites of birds,

Questioning the flight
of their migration,

Listening, but still
to question, alas,

Emptiness of songs,
frailty of wings,

On and on and on
until spring itself,

As such, becomes no
more of what it was,

And April, a thing
of the calendar.

iv.

The day seems motion-
less, but it is you,

Motionless under
the soft rain, weeping

Silently. Tremors
from another life

Reverberating
in your consciousness.

You peer through the bent
veneers of morning

And think, Sunday, so
classical, not jazz.

The street lamp flickers
itself on again

In the overcast
haze. Inclement

Vapors on the verge
of material.

The weather somehow
seems out of season

Or somehow out of
its own element

As if such a thing
were quite possible.

v.

You proceed your day,
with new incentives.

Recover from the
former night's routine.

Bring out a Heath bar
and the new Harper's.

Streets sublimated
gray and glistening,

The drizzle landing
in your coffee cup,

And your spectacles
spotted with rain drops.

This city and its
millions of people,

Masses turning through
the iron gateways.

Space invaders climb
the edge of buildings

Tiled in subversion,
an urban message

From the underground
and from up above.

vi.

So noiselessly in
your turbulent void

You stood and waited.
And there, in waiting

You somehow became
that stilted moment,

The fissure between
two possible worlds,

But one never to
actualize in time.

[VI]

i.

The mind is likened
to something unnamed,

An ineffable,
if not incognate.

What is there to show
for this anyway?

In variations
of a restless thought

The self will descend
in permutations.

It will traverse first
this way, then that way,

Until all learning
inchoate, unwinds,

Returning to their
respective bookends.

ii.

What is the measure
of your intellect?

—By one foolish act
after another?

The gathered pairs of
your precious workings,

Strange assemblage of
wanting and contempt–

There must be a word,
or words, to describe

This disposition
irreparable.

It would be quaint, a
quick roll of the tongue.

A formation of
two short, simple sounds.

This, that–so and so.
An iambic foot

Metered to end all
babble from here on.

iii.

The perfect object
sculpted, void collapsed,

The last word written,
shrill, illegible,

The final image
painted, a shadow

Exposed on the wall
darkly diffusing,

The final model
outlined and released

From the marble block,
the finality

Of a form conceived,
null, vicarious.

The architecture
of something absent,

Regard it, how? It
defies the maker

And the visceral
space it occupies.

iv.

And yet what if one
incoherent night

This improbable
thing were to occur?

Would I be prepared
for that encounter,

The chance meeting with
my alter ego?

The id becomes ill
in introspection,

The silent twin of
an upset culture

Back to avenge the
crimes against the self.

[VII]

i.

Stern, intent. Stern and
quite high with intent,

Now you sit, now stand,
rise and pace again.

Are you well prepared?
The course of events

To unfold will take
you to the limits

Of this contrivance.
It will displace you

In so many ways
—will dispossess you.

ii.

Fate is the way thought
to be its escape.

It is that hidden
place to where we flee,

A ventriloquist's
voice, elsewhere perceived,

Heard everywhere but
from his muted tongue.

Least expected–less
expected than that.

But you knew better,
undriven to act.

*A fish caught out on
dry land will struggle*

*With itself, but, for
being one alone,*

*It will not contest,
for well, it cannot.*

One must yield to force,
naturally–an act

Of necessity,
not of will. And yet,

In spite of force, you
will this all the same.

iii.

*I thought that with these
trembling lips might shape*

*The speech. Was it not
entirely in vain?*

*These repetitions
of bloom, meaningless,*

*Like the foliage
recurring as bound,*

*Eternally through
exertion, repose,*

*At first malignant
and still strangely kind,*

*Tearing the heart and
obscuring the mind*

*In the quiet night
against the seasons*

*Which come forth only
to expire. Behold,*

*The leaves have achieved
their repetition.*

*But what of the trees,
Mephistopheles,*

*The repetition
in which, with the leaves*

*Repeating, they them-
selves cannot achieve?*

*What divinity
bestows is fleeting.*

Hence its true beauty,
Doctor Faust, divine,

But you are blinded
by the haunt of fate.

For you are one to
whom this life decrees

The knowledge and the
pain, the wisdom too

With pain—all things, but
never without pain.

Compassion cannot
fathom this pathos.

—*So I am fated.*
Speak no more of fate.

The sun stands—the sun
standing. So it is,

The leafless branch sways
in terror, swaying,

And the mindless winds
brush over the grass.

Beyond these hills no
promise of such land

But the land that swears
to sustain exile.

You know well, to know
fate is to will it.

iv.

*In the waning course
of this afternoon,*

*I am reminded
of the simple things,*

*Things handed to the
hidden history.*

*Perhaps it is all
about letting go,*

*This life, our time here
aboriginal.*

*As born of a poem,
love, vague and untrue.*

*It does not seem to
have to be this way.*

And yet you harbor
this apprehension.

Towards the end of your
reflection you are

Employing a strange
kind of equation.

Sometimes we simply
need to say, out loud,

This is my abode.
It is cheap, unsound,

But I will not let
animals raze it.

Second to weakness
is your hesitance.

In this interval
of sublime silence

Centuries may pass.
Pause. Rewind. Play it

Back in slow motion:
A boy plants a tree.

The tree outlives him.
O, what brevity!

[VIII]

i.

Why is there nothing
rather than something?

That is the question.
The stasis of an

Ill-determinant.
We are like the wild.

We are all dying.
There is solace in

The fate unthwarted.
We are almost there.

ii.

Over sands will the
sea extend itself,

On to rocks the sea
exerting its own

With its waves, as if
each one were the last,

Dashing against stone.
Coastal winds will blow

With the scent of salt,
and presentiment

Of loss will hover
in the heavy night.

The air will linger
there uncertainly

And the moon will first
wax, then wane again

In indecision,
and the impromptu

Of birds in darker,
more distant jetties

Will into the night
air expand. Your skin,

Coarse like barnacles.
Coastal winds will blow

And finalities
will repeat themselves,

Each one quite distinct
from the one before.

Let the water shape
the rocks, there is time.

iii.

*I have taken that
walk along the shore*

*Watching the dark clouds
suspended above.*

*Only against stars
did they seem to move.*

*I held out my arms,
but they carried on.*

*Could I interject
with my strident song?*

*I watched the stray gulls
dipping into sea.*

*Would that a small part
remain for recall.*

*I remembered then,
thinking to myself,*

*Tonight, I shall die
that death once again.*

*Four and twenty years,
but what will happen?*

Quid pro quo, Doctor.
I give; you give back.

What do you wish? What
can it be that lies

Between your wanting
and your happiness?

Power? Knowledge? Or
perhaps simply love?

If only you knew,
how near you would be!

But no, indulgent
in the tragedy

To which you were born,
you insist upon

Distancing in the
face of that garden.

iv.

Take for instance this
trust: Concern the eye,

And the face blackened
by false promises.

The tale is tattered
of its own telling.

You have lived a life
of recollection.

I am free to choose.
—Free? You are not free.

A thing of the past
from which you might rise.

You have now become
but a memory

Of stolen years, its
absence, strangely like

An anchor released
to the changing sea.

Still you stoke the gaze
aflame, questioning.

You wish to be free.
We are of like mind.

We are without blame—
you and I, brothers.

What you wish and what
I seek in return

Are one and the same.
A pact can be made.

v.

If life were indeed
a stage, what player,

What motivating
force found from within

Would tell us how to
be, how to become?

This tragedy will
not contrive a script.

This was and is, and
will forever be

The greater clause of
your constitution.

Would it not be quite
outside of yourself?

There are poets, and
then, there are *poets*.

And you are among
them both equally.

How could you do this
by night and by day

Live that existence
quite ordinary?

Darkly translucent
and voluminous

Like a shadow the
walls could not contain,

The night will yield a
little for measure.

Pride knows but one curb,
and this be not proud.

Again you play out
that old illusion.

The lifeless teachings
posit their meanings

Vacant of any
real experience.

These affectations
cannot restore us.

Neither idea,
nor the thing either,

Both of which are of
little importance.

*I have been given
the eyes of a muse*

*And yet, not its tongue.
This reads injustice.*

*I say it again,
"I know nothing," and*

*The cold irony
slips like the hemlock*

*Drunk of resistance,
a still death without*

*Much transformation
in which to find gain,*

*A symposium
where convenes accord.*

The same reflected
image in the sky

Reflected in our
eyes, so projected.

*Troubled and flightless
again this body.*

–A dead man unearthed
by the harsh god-head

To whom we might owe
the greatest account.

[IX]

i.

The heavens contend
for their permanence.

What a thousand years
of progress the gods

Will not consort to
shatter in a tear

By the lithe letting
of a human eye.

Forever unchanged
–immutable this.

Choice upon choice, or
the long series of

Indecisions, when
comes the day we stand,

Our faces swollen
with apprehension.

And on that day all
things will be revealed.

Without the pretense
of any yielding,

It will proceed to
annihilate us.

ii.

It must have been here.
Or, if not, a place

Much like this. A place
without suffrage.

And it must have been
a night like this one.

The ready moon poised
in the naked sky,

The stars abounding
with intimations.

What congregation
of people found here

So singular a
motive, this force formed?

What foreign commerce
and trade traversed here?

How many years to
build these twin towers,

With their ministries
and their undoings?

And so we shall make
history complete.

We shall close the ring
and begin again,

Contrive a point to
which all things converge.

[X]

i.

Inquire the muse: What
begins at the end

But the beginning
of another end,

Another forming
of a postulate?

Things that cannot last
will seldom stay long.

This much has been learned.
Beyond this, what more?

Even half and half
cannot make the whole.

Lives and happiness
shall never marry.

We have gotten lost.
We are everything

That has gotten lost.
We sigh. Who believes

To have found their way?
They, too, remain lost

In the labyrinth
of thousands of years.

ii.

It was the way in
which I was chosen.

The borrowed language
had itself an air

Of incompleteness.
But without it, there

Would have been nothing.
Could time start over

Things would be different.
Martyr this moment,

This difficult task.
I am not the one.

Another will come
later, more learned

And more inspired
for yet another

Metamorphosis.
Greater achievement.

A little higher,
for a time longer.

To take one's own life
by all that is good.

The hour long since passed,
and leaves no longer

Leaves, since relinquished.
Like queries lost to

The vast indifference,
so too these longings

Irreverent against
the turbulent sky.

To want to know, to
want to feel again

The life, the living,
not this insolvent

Reminiscence, this
backward extension.

iii.

Say that the world is
not a catalogue

Of inequities.
Down without recoil.

It is no grave thing,
this disparity.

The days, no longer
what had been premised.

Some essence achieved
but not transmitted.

Confide, can nothing
be done properly?

But still like a small
provision, the sun

Rises, the sun sets,
and the air imports

Curious in the
changing of seasons.

iv.

What do I know of
anything, really?

Colorless it comes
without appointment

Only to reside
a while among us.

The remains remain.
How shall I go on?

It has only taught
me how to forget.

The courage to say
I am a person

And the patience to
wait it out, longer.

Seamless counterpart,
Surrogate wonders.

What is sadness but
the sense of these things?

Widely convinced of
the excessiveness,

Willingness itself
becomes unwilling

In orchestration.
The infinitude

Of a single thought,
the ending of which

We are not to know.
Better to not have

At all, whatever
one may think of next.

Better for recall.
Better to sever.

v.

You will remark as
genuine, the loss.

And beauty occurs
solely in the mind.

Rest not eminent
nor love eternal,

These notions have been
well documented,

Appended here, with
enigmatic light.

What say you to this,
speechless companion?

Instructing motions
of doubt and doubting.

Extraordinary
these changes, and yet

How life remains life-
less in the same ways.

Luckless souvenir,
noting nothing new,

How unhappiness
like a dog, loiters.

It has followed me
through the alley ways,

To all the places
I go, when I go.

vi.

Having thus become
learned in all things

The long lesson of
unlearning begins.

Try to mystify
this ill-fittedness

Which is no longer
of much mystery.

The perceived shifting
of the ocean's weight

For instance, or the
discovery of

The reflexiveness
in being aware.

The discovery
of discovery,

Of self-awareness,
and the knowing all.

A wish to be free
of account, a wish

To be just that, and
simply so. To be

Out of context from
any incident,

The man behind the
shadow of the man,

The auxiliary
to the mise-en-scène.

Immunity from
the arbiter's reach,

Distance accorded
with clear distinction.

To be present at
the intersecting

Winds, and bear witness
to the strange kairos

So to be free of
doubt, and too, of faith.

A wish to see all
so to see not more.

A wish to sit still
and be, as it were.

But where is the will?
This divided life

Has not an ending
nor a beginning.

vii.

So it is said with
careful instruction

Knowledge is the prime
of acquisitions.

It is possible.
But I shall say this:

Self-knowledge that one
must remain without,

Foreknowledge that true
knowledge does not come,

And that wisdom does
not gain from its own,

Is the one thing known.
This much and no more.

There is no access
to that cool comfort

For the luxury
is beyond getting.

viii.

Could it be spoken
and still be? Could I

Achieve a sound more
subtle than ourselves?

Like the troubled sky,
black night unto blue,

Blue unto purple,
unto magenta.

And so uncertain
of the cause it goes.

To have lost all thought
of the epitaph,

Evading any
compulsion to strike.

And really, it seems
to go well this way

That the time spent in
kerning seems fruitless.

The beauty of the
word, the paradigm

Of language. And yet
what is this to me,

The quintessence of
verbiage? No, drama

Delights not me, nor
poetry neither.

Though by your smiling—
Forgive me, Doctor.

ix.

You have been privy
to the disclosure

Of the will and of
the way made by it.

And it may be so.
But I shall say this:

The self-same callous
hand that turns the page

Snuffs the candle's flame.
Half and half contend

To contrive madness.
You are innocent.

You know but one half.
—I do not know much.

x.

I have fallen in
to illness of late,

An illness only
a mother could mourn.

Something has gone wrong.
Why it is this way

I shall never know.
Without having sworn,

So many times I
said things to myself

I was wanting to
believe, but could not.

This flame here, Wagner,
see how it flickers

At the slightest wind.
I hover my hand

Over it and watch
how quietly it

Burns, so quietly
like an anxious heart

Summoned to be still.
But still, shivering

By the sliver of
fear that twists the night.

This flame rises like
the lifting pages

Of a book deafened
by its very words.

This flame smolders like
a resumed spirit

At once ascending
and descending, too

As if another
by its consumption

Might rise anew from
its smothered embers.

More light, and the moth
shall render itself.

Revealed at this time
in full disclosure

I shall learn too well
this fire is contained

Only in the mind.
Like the dim glow of

The evening's end, it
burns not bright, nor long.

xi.

Many have spoken
duly proclaiming

This and that, but now
witness otherwise:

Time present, time past,
and time soon to come,

Subjunctive in them-
selves, conditional,

Are contained in one
another's presence.

All things are therefore
at once arriving,

Departing, if not
eternally still.

Retrievable then,
the mutable past

Despite what one has
conjectured before.

By its tenants we
have recognized it.

*Mere desire without
much strength manifest*

*Supposes this lack
of something needed.*

Supposing then all
reciprocities

Collapse inert, for
it seems to be so.

I wish to live but
I have not the strength.

Shall I wage my way
against the seasons

Which impend so to
redeem those now lost?

Half and half make up
this divided self.

xii.

This relic is not
mine yet declares to

Make me who I am
in the reduction

Of such constancy.
Folded into hands

I take this trifle
into my being,

Make precise like pain,
toll for the tolling.

How much longer now,
this moment maligned?

Permit me this fault,
corrective callous.

It was in my blood
forming otherwise.

The misanthrope would
emerge from the world

Well meaning but turned
in the harsh day light,

Carried here broken
to this nameless place.

Weightless as wanting
I drift spiritless

Through the old remnants
weaving a story

Of suffered objects
I shall never tell.

I will commit the
secret sacrifice

Until I have seen
the consummate bind.

In host of many
such atrocities,

Implacable form
abridged for regret,

Where begins the deep
grieving–forty days

And forty slow nights
teeming on themselves.

It is raining now.
So it seems to rain

Always. This solemn
melancholy lasts,

Sustaining itself.
The constant sound draws

My ear, I listen.
I take in the air.

The odor of flesh
when it is storming

Preserves me from sleep.
I gaze to the streets.

My senses will not
forsake me, this time.

xiii.

*Call this a solstice
seldom if ever,*

*Perhaps a harvest
moon that might have been.*

*People never met,
places never seen,*

*Ultimate voyeur
to another life,*

*Indeed, these affairs
so vicarious.*

*So closely do you
scrutinize this pain.*

*You have re-opened
the scar, Doctor Faust.*

*And with one hand you
examine the wound*

*Unwitting of the
hand that holds the knife.*

What is sought in life
shall only be found

In death. Argument,
the revisioning

Without protocol,
neither with epode.

They are to be marked.
You will remember

The blood of this truce
spilling on the page.

"Leave all hope, you who
enter," it is said.

Deny that treason,
that great temptation.

It is danger, more,
it is madness. This

Foreboding cannot
wake its weight enough.

I do not claim to
know much, but I know

The slow hand you hold
in the fire will burn.

*No victor can rise
out of this struggle.*

*The final light will
forsake all reason.*

THE SECOND QUARTER

[XI].

i.

Much apprehension
brought about stillness

And the dark. Listless
longings cast upward

To surrogate skies,
wanton, left to chance.

Whatever desires
without form and dazed

Immaterial
like apparitions

Never to arrive
for the beholder.

What of this night? What
of this constant rain?

And the moon with its
malicious intent?

*The falling rain is
not unlike that of–*

ii.

These four walls of raw
steel, cinder, and stone,

Crude with jagged nails,
once pulled, now breaking,

Define the space, where
overhead at night

Mysterious pipes
run water and gas

Charting out clatter
in constellations.

Nocturnal engines
that steam and stammer

Like chambers of a
mind ill at its ease,

Turning, turning in
a strange habitat.

iii.

Study the figure
flanked and racked awake,

Though paler and less
tender, so sanguine.

Aware, with ribs like
hands pushing through skin.

A generation
of recovered scars

Pulsating as to
burst again. Regard

The knotting of the
exposed spine, naked

To the circumstance
of cement floors. Torn

Muscles tautened and
made whiter than bone,

And what blood flows, flows
deeper than marrow.

Tired eyes follow the
flies buzzing around,

Nail them to walls but
still they keep moving.

iv.

How many are there
lying sleeplessly

Beyond closed shutters?
Lives pressed against walls,

And turning yellow
by the old curtains

In attendance of
the late messenger.

*Though not on this day
perhaps on the next.*

They have cut you off
on utilities.

You sit in the dark
with a candlelight.

Bad diplomacy.
Life without pension.

So you have done it
(and with such daring).

Murdered happiness,
married misery.

Something about this
tragically endures.

Hours brought together
in complicity

For what seemed something
short of completeness.

Eyes no longer eyes
before the object.

These words surrender.
They release their sounds.

v.

The soft rain murmurs
of the loneliness.

The street lamp shines a
dizzy cone of light

Illuminating
the mist and the haze.

What the night devours...
you could walk for hours.

vi.

The diner flips its
sign and locks its door.

The last swamper, done,
takes a bar stool down,

Rolls a cigarette,
takes out a folded

Postcard he received.
He keys a half-song

On the piano.
He shuts out the lights.

By the wet sidewalk
mindless of the rain

He waits for the train
to take him elsewhere.

Suddenly, darkness
overwhelms. The wind

Dies hush. Suddenly,
the silence presides.

What the night devours.
These are the streets you

Walk, the same corners
by which you stop and

Stand, before turning
unto an unknown.

[XII]

i.

They did not tell you
the price of squatting,

Not of the toothless
and unabashed hound

Irreverently in
the alley barking,

Nor of ghosts breaking
glass by the dumpsters.

This peevish unrest
of an anxious night

Tosses you side to
side, and up again.

It has you looking
out to the sidewalks

Waiting for a clue,
an indication

Of something other,
perhaps something more.

ii.

*I received the goods,
and thank you again.*

*I apologize
for the frequent and*

*Importune requests
coming from my end.*

*You did not realize
you would hence be named*

*The guardian of
my worthless estate.*

You left school thinking
you could do better.

Strung out on Prozac,
nocturnally prone,

You thought of other
possibilities.

All your college friends
were getting married,

Graduating in
Law or Medicine,

Moving to bigger
and brighter cities,

Leasing new Volvos
and buying condos.

Sooner or later
(a matter of time)

You would seek out their
pro bono service.

They would walk you through
your Chapter 7.

They would look after
your stomach tumor.

This was the city
where you had once lived.

These were the people
with whom you exchanged.

The losers you hung
with in coffee shops,

Where are they now, these
fugitives of sleep?

The alcoholics
and all the retards

At the half-way house
with a deck of cards

—But half-way to what?
Trying to survive,

Seldom embarking,
never to arrive.

iii.

*I have brought to life
some forty sonnets*

*On this typewriter
with a missing e,*

*One for each long day,
and each endless night.*

*By this broken hand
I have taken lines*

*Strung them together
for the homage of*

*Dear Persephone,
musings refined by*

*The sharpness of light,
ported by candles,*

*Drunk from the vessel,
and rendered inert.*

It was you, nameless
and without a way,

The confused moiré
of the evening's wake

Full of static and
neon, full of haste.

The hustle and heist,
the shuffle and go,

The detriment of
a grave digression

Through the slow twist of
a dead end standing.

All the terrible
motors of midnight

Like the resonance
of a misplayed note,

A motion made to
outdistance the stars.

iv.

You had visions of
pigeons fluttering

Through the bay windows
in the hidden room,

Raising marble dust
into shafts of light,

Nesting in the brick
oven corridors,

Perched on the sewage
pipes since sweated dry.

You gathered the shards
of the broken glass,

And with blood stained hands
declared your domain,

Mapped the mosaic
upon which to lie.

Somewhere lost in the
abandonment was

The pretext of a
painter poised for death,

Only to awake
without redemption.

[XIII]

i.

Sitting and waiting.
Waiting and sitting.

Sitting and waiting
in the erosion,

Finally standing
to calmly exit.

An erosion from
the indifference,

An erosion from
the madness. *Bebop,*

*Hiphop, nose pop and
eye drop.* The madness.

*Vintage shops, subway
stops, traffic cops, and*

Urban props. Madness,
from all the madness.

What the night inflicts,
the day knows nothing.

ii.

Madness is the fear
of a woman's touch.

Madness is the fear
before the desire.

Madness is the fear
anticipated,

A maddened sort of
climactic illness.

Madness is the fear
of a fear undone.

Fear of fear of fear.
Fear of madness. *Cheap*

*Thrills, land fills, bar spills,
buzz kills.* Madness is.

*Moonlit hills, broken
mills, and window sills.*

This landscape tells no-
thing of history,

As if this climate,
down on your dismay.

*Written page, gilded
cage and narrow stage—*

How terrible, you
are so far from home.

*Long goodbyes, angel
eyes and no disguise....*

You are here on this
metropolitan

Morning, still as a
stone, a cigarette

Dangling dry in your
lips, the newspaper

Classifieds flapping
in the wind, your face,

A woodcut weathered.
What the poet hears,

*The painter sees. Or
so the poet says.*

*There seems no meaning
beyond this masked face.*

iii.

Today, today is
the first day–the last.

This is your life. This
is the commencement

Of your life, the rest
of your life. Today

Is the rest of your
life. And yesterday–

Yesterday is out,
already lost now,

Fully lost to the
waywardness of things.

Yesterday was lost
to a memory,

Lost like yesterday,
lost like the many

Yesterdays now lost
to the waywardness.

Incessantly lost
in forgetfulness.

iv.

You rented a damp
basement apartment,

And built this bivouac
between two brownstones.

Bought a frying pan
and some window shades,

And a broken lamp
to illuminate

The rites. You laid back
to regard your site

While the rainbow trout
was marinating

In the vinaigrette
with sesame grounds.

Waiting for Godot,
a table for one.

*We have come too far
ignoring knowledge.*

*Lost, we shall wander
over the remains.*

*Lost—let it pass, let
it pass lost, I say.*

–For infectious was
the losing of it,

So complete in its
curiosity.

v.

Usurped units of
disposable time

Cascaded in a
stream of consciousness.

And so it followed,
and nobody knew.

You made abstract move-
ments in abstractions.

The hand covering
the face, the face turned.

Today is the first
day. This is your life.

*The noisy jazz and
beer in smoke filled rooms,*

*And the relentless
dreams the night resumes...*

*All this I presume
to be the endless*

*Derivatives sought
in the hour recessed*

*Between two poems,
anxious, scattered by*

False imperatives.
Time spun itself down

And the days unwound.
It was a myth, this

Life, this existence.
Today is the day....

vi.

*The infinitely
complex subtleties*

*Involved, involving
us, the bare knowledge*

*In contradiction
to understanding,*

*The singular hold,
a motion to move,*

*And the infinite
commotion therein,*

*The slightest notion
of a sleight of hand*

*Now forever lost.
We begin, we end.*

*Who can say? We are
like the mustard seeds*

*Waylaid and adrift
by the weeds and thorns.*

vii.

You emptied them all,
the bottles of songs,

A kind of numbness
unto death's respite,

Biting down on salt
and throwing Cuervo

Until dawn when you
found yourself alone

And so utterly
within the confines

Of your own construct,
stenching of raw fish.

What did it matter?
No one could touch you.

You were so cool. You
were so fucking cool

In the dark vortex
of your solitude.

[XIV]

i.

Galleries, restaurants,
hair salons, hotels,

(Tip the fedora
to the maître d')

Vintage clothes boutiques
and Victor Hugo

Avenue book store,
browse the used and rare,

The first editions
and the out of prints,

Or try on a pair
of shoes at Fluevog,

Then be on your way.
Down Newbury Street,

Arlington, Berkeley,
Clerendon, Dartmouth,

Exeter, Fairfield,
Gloucester, and Hereford,

You will chart them all
back to the Common.

Stroll the promenade
for a while, perhaps

Skip a few pebbles
into the water.

Then up Beacon Hill
past the loading docks,

The State Capitol,
and the Parker House,

Make a quick pass through
the Union graveyard.

ii.

Spare change find their way
to a stranger's cup.

A blind accordion
slackens, and then swoons.

The hands conjecture
their own reflection

Against a window.
A lit cigarette

Suspends the traffic.
You think it over.

The urban passions
of a vacant lot

And the nights expunged
of their high purpose.

The promise of a
street corner at night

On a cement bench,
the separation

In six degrees of
such proximity.

Boston, the people
and traffic, been there,

In cafés with drinks
and small talk, done that.

Public restrooms head-
line the latest tricks.

The graffiti jazz.
The cobble stone waltz.

Redline over Charles,
Harvard Square Cambridge,

Finger on the pulse,
by the public phones,

Ticket agency
and Out of Town News.

A cup of coffee
for a game of chess.

iii.

This city built stone
upon stone, you see,

The people christened
patron, citizen,

Towers erected
out of enterprise,

Machines of power,
industry and war.

Innocent, you think
of a Roman coin

With its face eaten
off by centuries

Burning wild like a
stigma in your hand.

Give unto Caesar.
But what is Caesar's?

iv.

You came with prospects
of profound reward,

Returned once more to
this decisive place.

Paradise, exiled
from another life,

Forever far and
vanishing again.

The failure of years,
the respective pomp,

Lessons refuted
unlearned by deaf ears,

The prodigal son
returns without love.

He is admitted
but not reconciled.

He is forgiven
but not understood.

And the mother you
never took to heart

Would still be waiting
with arms extended

Outstretching the full
distance that you fled.

v.

You watched the signals,
You felt them changing:

The tin can clunking
along the street curb,

The tattered awnings
flapping their wide wings,

The washed out billboards
rain-stripped and streaking.

You were motionless
and high in the drone

Of the asphalt sky.
You were quite alone.

The colors of red
and green flickering,

The condensation
of the darkening.

You stood there perplexed
in the tight traffic,

Sedated within
the imperfection

Of sense, divested
of all enterprise,

Uninfected by
the clamor and cause.

Tied to your being,
you were confounded.

You could not decide.
You stood there frozen.

Thus was inertia,
so you should not move,

So you should not think
of yourself moving.

[XV]

i.

Four A.M. Soon the
breath of birds will sound.

First a cigarette,
and some black coffee.

Then more cigarettes.
Affected motions

Repetitious, un-
reasoned. Compulsive.

*All this packing
and unpacking.*

Contemplative and
curious the smoke

Rises and expands
filling the new light.

*The song that carries
dawn stirs the silence.*

*The day emerging
blinds in white fury.*

*And I am made wit-
less in agony*

*To know the coming
of another day*

*And made deaf to all
the signs of morning.*

ii.

The mythology
of a race plays out,

Lying recumbent
inhaling toxins

On the floors of un-
furnished studios,

Wasting themselves with
the radio on,

Muttering words that
dribble out so spent.

But you knew better.
Greatness envisioned,

Things would be different.
Articulate words

Would soon form to speech.
Echoing excess,

You thought by then you
would be justified,

Doubting cogencies
of generations.

This narrative would
walk you through the mire

Of mitigation.
And you knew better

To trace backwardly
that primitive pride.

iii.

The sun shimmers through
the broken window

In the form of a
thief bearing a flame.

Eastwardly you face
to embrace the day,

To abound in the
poverty of warmth

And to behold what
little life is deigned.

You had searched them all.
Perhaps by then you

Knew each name by face.
Catalogue this place

As the alternate
among the others.

Naked you entered
later to return

In happiness or
in envy thereof.

It was only then
that you saw the past

(Whereof in envy)
the light of the dawn

Slowly betraying
the truth of that time.

[XVI]

i.

You told me I smelled
like your grandfather.

It was the cigar
smoke in the tweed coat.

You meant it in the
best possible sense

Of course, and I said
that it was all right.

And we, being young, half
danced to the music.

But then you kissed my
neck and I got lost.

ii.

And did I know it
then, that years later

I would trace again
and anticipate

With tears which could not
form at first, but would,

Through affectations
derived of seasons

And the grand gestures
of the open sky,

All the weighed wishes
of the twilight moon,

The windowpanes rain
streaked with memories

So murmurously
dark with my desire?

iii.

Burgundy, cognac,
tobacco and pipe.

The jacket hanging
on the music stand.

The dignity of
years settled in debt.

The classic tales bound
in attic leather,

Indispensable
to the library.

These archives invent
aristocracy.

Dark mysteries contained
in the wooden chest,

A time capsule of
an aging culture.

The letters wrapped in
brown paper and tied,

The cracked picture frame,
the photo album

And prints aging in
their own sepia.

The family of five
in immigrant wool,

Each with hair neatly
parted on the side.

And could they see me
I would wave to them.

iv.

The torch that passes
through generations

A frightened flame, wind-
whipped and flickering,

The heir apparent
and inheritor

Of weight, of struggle
to uphold a name,

A face grown older
by its heritage.

These thing are not real.
They do not exist.

v.

Pull the shade open.
The cracking of light

Softly awakens
the latent notes of

Sunday sonatas
which your sister played.

You will breath in the
frescoes and the oils.

You will stroke the stretched
canvas with your hand.

This will mark the plan
at its origin.

In still life, all would
be much clearer then.

Soon all would have their
place and be defined.

vi.

The sleight of witting
stance that shifts unseen,

And the forming of
that surmising smile,

A glint in the eye
becomes a glitter.

You pose in the glass
and it reflects back

Vanity, the lack
and the emptiness

From which you swore to
preempt with pigments,

Oils thick as mortar
on palette and knife.

vii.

Perhaps you had come
in search of something?

Swaddled unsafe in
your adolescence

You stood there, the edge
of this hidden place.

Your memory brought
you back divided

And upset. Tortured
with footing unsure,

You stopped to ponder
the distancing stretch

Of this privileged path.
There was nowhere left.

You for whom nothing
hitherto was clear,

Knew you would never
henceforth be certain.

viii.

And at the fireplace
a crematory,

The ashes of the
manuscript you burned.

You let it burn, made
that the tragedy.

And in your veins you
felt it surge at last,

The blood purged of that
regrettable past.

You left that place and
its memories behind.

Did that fire incite
your twice backward gaze?

You turned away and
paused beside the door

To contemplate your
passage out again.

But then you were free.
Like the new water

Coursing the wasted
furrows of dead streams,

You had found your way
and resumed your life.

[XVII]

i.

This is God's country,
South seeking solstice

On roads leading no
where, crossing nothing.

But today, there are
two suns in the sky

With heat hung arid
over the asphalt.

The migraine of a
wasted afternoon

Like a bayonet
driving derelict.

Pray for the rain, pray
for the day to end.

ii.

A map, a duffel
bag, a change of clothes,

A few toiletries
and a will to roam.

You drove without fear,
without possession,

Only the landscape
borrowed for the day.

The rearview mirror
deflected the road

Behind you and so
no one could catch you.

iii.

Motels and diners,
gas station rest stops

With cigarettes and
a water bottle.

As meaningless as
the days of the week,

Everything reduced
to this one moment,

A disk of light like
a coin, clenched and placed

Carefully in your
pocket for recall.

Thus you had fallen
from that paradise.

Each destination
claimed its own vector

But everywhere seemed
the very essence

Of somewhere quite lost,
of nowhere founded.

iv.

In the recluse of
rivers by a bend

Where a tree leans in
to the water's bank

A fire will ascend.
You saw the raven

Perched on its nest of
pomp. A broken bough

Against the wind, and
against everything.

So instruct the light
in what respite, the

Significant sigh,
the causality

In each caustic cry,
cleaved by consequence.

Twice and twice the red
crocodile will wield

New wisdom expelled
of its appetite.

You will shake the rose
of its steel petals.

A finger will then
untwist this season

Out of the wind, so
out of everything.

v.

No expectancy.
This pealed Polaroid

Slide reveals the blood
of the slain sparrow.

Your heart will quiver
a little as you

Gaze through the smoke with
eyes defiled by dust.

Pray for the rain, pray
for the day to end.

Such solace exceeds
nothing of the pain

Against this wind—or
against anything.

Pray for the rain, pray
for this day to end.

[XVIII]

i.

You might begin with
this alteration:

A door swings into
a darkened corner.

Too much of what once
was hardly enough,

Never right. Seldom
spoken. Disbelief.

And windless, the flags.
I am so frightened

By the world and its
infinite intrigue.

Repeat after me.
From my window I

See the freights passing.
I can hear them roar.

ii.

Shall I describe it
to you? How the rage

Displaced the very
feeling it evoked?

Evocation of—
Between desire and

The object stretches
infinite expanse.

This I learned too late.
This tongue difficult

And unassuming,
the important stare

Fixes brilliant eyes.
The terror of torn

Colors incognate,
dissonant unto

The wind in reply.
And meanwhile in some

Other latitude,
insomnia and jazz.

This nostalgia the
scenery accords.

iii.

I had an idea
of the new order.

To know again what
once was forgotten—

Quite frankly, it was
neither here nor there.

But then, it was of
vaporous content.

Little consequence.
Destined for downfall,

Like the contortions
of an alleged fear.

Devised for greatness,
deranged of that same

Disillusionment.
Genius is the sure

Precursor for that
thing we call madness.

iv.

He came from Boston
working on a book,

The semiotics
of the subjunctive,

The ontology
of fools, so it seemed.

He wanted to start
up a coffee shop,

A late night hangout
for the derelicts.

He would often speak
in the third person.

v.

The analysis
of finite feelings

In the final hour,
in the deep recess

The sound made larger
and more distorted.

Eclectic birds with
their elated songs,

The stock quotations,
the medical charts.

Take them from the im-
pound to the psych ward.

I am the shadow
of my enemy.

I am the shadow
of my own being.

vi.

It was about the
lingering remnants,

The laughter, and the
moment just after.

Quite certain it was
not of much substance,

Summer was a short
suspension drifting.

Truffles and hot tea,
the three-minute steep,

Lazy afternoons
through open windows.

You did not think it
possible at first.

You had learned it well,
to bury yourself

With happiness, with
free and guiltless bliss.

It's quite all right. You
are experiencing

Difficulties. This
is only a test.

If this had been a
real emergency

Situation, you'd
be in pain just now.

[XIX]

i.

The evening terrace
delivers the view

Of the summer's end.
You, with sunglasses

And tea, add an hour
to the twilight breeze.

Wicker and linen
abide with sandals

Upraised on the stone
slate of the fountain.

ii.

The lantern flickers
to retain the light,

Permeation of
this incandescence.

In silent shades of
the darkening sky,

First Hesper, then the
rest, one after one

Until a closed dome
of sorrow suspends

The heavy mood and
the crickets pervade

The beechwood and tile.
Without much warning,

This is how the days
segue into nights.

iii.

Too long since you have
regarded these things,

The rumination
of such reluctance.

You retrieve the stray
stories with a pen

And live the cahier
of another life.

All that you can to
this transparent end.

But really, is this
what you had in mind?

Your thoughts are swaying.
And so you grace through

Like a song of a
mid-western county.

Perhaps you shall wake
tomorrow and be

That man you had sworn
to be. Perhaps not.

So little seems to
turn out as you plan.

iv.

A bird is nesting
in the pergola.

A willow leans in
to the shade and weeps.

*I know this now, I
am but a poet.*

*All else for me has
been despite my being.*

Meanwhile the pages
flutter out of sight

Like white pigeons chased
by a bicycle.

*Would that a moment
arise out of time,*

*The interstices
in rhyme untelling,*

*That I should sit and
wait in the winding*

*Of another day,
another cleaving.*

*For I, have I not
wasted myself dear?*

v.

Condensations of
the night, in endless

Hours a magenta
gently permeates

With waning light, and
everywhere, shadows.

A sky so vast one
can drown. So quickly

Now the dominion
of a viscous black.

Where in the absence
of such otherness,

Day or night, can we
seek to find something

Containing a bit
of something other?

This occurrence of
the subtle and slight,

A tenderness that
moves, the rain that cools

The late evening would
evoke this desire.

vi.

It would be a night
like this, would it not?

If not in silence,
you would speak a word

And then join it with
another, elate,

A rapture which was
inevitable,

The passing of a
moment, bound in time,

Arrived of need, a
force, a will to be.

As if this city
and its circumstance

Were a stage set in
place for this one scene.

It would so happen
on a night like this.

vii.

The climate to which
you open yourself

Completely by chance
as you shift and shift

Your days and somehow
manage to remain

On the same routine
restores your body.

Morning will arrive
and you will be in

That crowded metro
replete with assholes,

Invalids, and bums
reeking of urine,

Sweat, and enterprise,
coffee mug in hand,

Sleep still in your eyes,
traversing tunnels

To round out the day,
square and meaningless

As the one before,
be it in uptown,

Downtown or central,
as Wall Street broker,

Investment banker,
and art director.

This is how you will
found your citadel.

Nostalgia, regret,
both, you would murder.

[XX]

i.

Pedantry turned a
palaver of rhymes,

Epistle verses,
letters never sent,

Leningrad, returned
postage, Palestine,

The ink dried and the
fountain pen's tip bent.

These are all that there
remain. Your study,

The safe partition
that you erected,

In extremities
devised, so exact.

ii.

The heavy brass hands
of the clock melt down

One to another
the countless hours

Which brood upon them-
selves, inscrutably.

This reclining chair,
this desk, this evening,

Tobacco and pipe,
conditioned coffee,

The metaphysics
of a jazz culture.

We are thus defined
by our surroundings.

We are defined by
our own negation

Of what we are not.
The present is but

A moment passing.
We are; we are not.

iii.

To express from the
editor's desk is,

To be sure, only
proverbial. You sit

Across the room from
your station. You see

The strewn papers, un-
promissory notes,

Pads and post-its of
yellow and of green,

Much like discolored
leaves shaken and stripped,

Sublimated through
the macchina fax.

A misplaced verse from
a secret sonnet,

And you think to your-
self looking about,

This room is like a
thousand other rooms

In Moscow, Paris,
Naples and Berlin.

This dialectic,
this seeing, behold:

The new model of
human consciousness,

The terra cotta
of your discontent,

If you will, contoured
modernist malaise.

iv.

You learned the exile's
edict word for word,

Raised a dais for
your recitation.

The speech you tendered
has turned on you and

Compelled you into
silence. Arbiter,

Claim no poppy for
your erring epic.

For legacy was
but a verse in time,

That line once drawn in
sand a wave erased.

Those distant coasts long
to be seen again.

v.

*Why is it like this
and not some other?*

An introspection
pronounced outwardly.

What is the point of
your questioning so?

A bowl of ripe fruit
with skin like leather

Placed on the table.
The scent of ginger

And sesame oil,
a hint of sadness

Fragrant in the halls
darkened by velvet.

Still-life of some kind
in contingent curves.

A glass on the verge
of beading awaits

Without history,
without inertia.

The pen is unmoved,
intelligence fled,

Lacking the essence
of imagining.

A prayer echoes
in empty chambers.

Where beauty begins
there ends the other.

vi.

In much overture
you light the candles.

You pour the coffee
and wait the night

In certain vigil.
Then a sudden pang.

Stiff like an old mime,
pensive like Pierrot,

You place the record
on the phonograph.

You needle it on
and then off again.

A breath is taken
and there is no sound.

You perceive yourself
in black and white stills.

Grainy, unfocused.
Forget all of this.

The elder voice of
a Russian poet

Would smother you in
wide oblivion.

vii.

Being here without
being quite present,

No more lamenting
things ephemeral.

The universe is
beyond affecting.

This I will have learned
before my last word.

So it starts with all
and ends with nothing.

Confounded without,
witless Dædalus,

Reckless passion has
succeeded the craft.

A higher craft now
needed to succeed

This passion, and so
another passion

To succeed again
this much higher craft–

On and on and on
until labyrinth

Lies impossible,
and flight absolute.

Whereas your art had
once kept you alive;

Whereas your art now
keeps you from living.

Tortured by nature,
poet and artist

By consequent course,
non-negotiable

Price exorbitant.
We lose, we all lose.

And like silhouettes
littering the light

They but recall the
dissipating words

And incantations
inert, the very

Litanies weathered
into nothingness.

Like the vision that
launched a thousand ships,

Abound in hubris,
ill fated passion.

The present is but
the moment passing

Between history
and our forgetting.

Then it will be said
of you and your ways

Here stands half a man
–half a will to stand.

INTERLUDE

[XXI]

i.

What are the contours
of these missing forms?

The outline achieved
in muted measures.

The proposed outcome
has not a meaning,

Endeavors not to
reveal anything.

ii.

A reading lamp
a pen, a piece of

Paper, a notion
plainly written out.

Nights can be pensive
at such late hours,

Alone but for the
effervescent ring.

You heed the calling,
renounce your nature

And make twice obscure
the unwanted gain,

This without-which-not
of haunting specters.

iii.

*Tell me if you know,
Mephistopheles,*

*Why, when the oil has
burned, the wax melted*

*And the wick consumed,
there is no remnant*

*Of light lingering?
Can you tell me this?*

*Why and whereof these
things occur, and how?*

One will furnish their
own reality.

But why so many
questions? *—And why not?*

—That, too, is it not
a kind of question?

iv.

*O, would that I could
without ways withheld*

*Relinquish here these
verses so to let*

*These words upon their
forming be dissolved*

*That I might find peace
in something other.*

*And would that I could
without speech ascend*

*To find heaven void
of humanity,*

*To hear the shrill sound
that shatters the sky,*

*Scattering us through
out the earth this time*

*Forever free of
hate and fear, I would.*

v.

So sad and strange for
us to meet like this,

With you sitting there
huddled with your tea,

Much less than subdued
in countenance,

Less than gaiety
in your trying smile.

Youthful faces pale
like premonitions

Recall: The slow sky
will stir and the rain

Will fall expressly
for those among us

Least inclined to talk
of such fair weather.

vi.

The holiday's din
with celebration

Seizes the room in
a haze of stale smoke.

And everything in
your field of vision

Becomes stilted like
a film staggering

Through a projector.
You come to realize

You can claim nothing
and that you remain

Faithfully your own
and vulnerable

In your innermost
being which persists

Like a bad tumor
despite everything.

You have followed it
through continents, but

All you see is the
black trail of demons.

vii.

*Would that in the dark
of hours I could*

*With lame and witless
hands create an edge*

*Immortal against
our eternal sphere,*

*All but to cease the
subtlety, I would,*

*All but to feel the
heavy stone and steel.*

–Strange, this questioning,
and your heart ablaze,

Then just as now, with
passion and despair.

No mysticism
I admit and yet

There is something in
this fire, something real.

A struck match makes it
all come back so clear.

See this candle here,
Doctor Faust. This light

Is like the hidden
star of Pleiades.

It is like Hesper.
This flame, it is like

Heaven and earth as
one, if you so choose.

Indeed, if you so
choose, it shall then be.

viii.

Never the truth; for
ever the context.

And almost always
with consequences.

What is this we call
life without freedom?

This cleaving and this
yearning need must end.

It does not kill, it
does not make stronger,

This hour adrift
between two unknowns.

Knowing knowledge ends
but in unknowing,

These eyes will conjure
without the vision

The profound summons
of incense and smoke.

ix.

This day is a day
like any other.

And yet, today, this
Second of July,

The very center
of the calendar,

This year of our lord
two thousand and four,

The consecration
of what is in store.

Whereas the wind swirls
about, indifferent,

It cares not and the
night concedes this breath.

Whereas the starless
sky assumes the dark.

And the moon trembles,
foreboding and pale.

In short, this evening
is ill at its ease.

Whereas this hoping
is lost in despair.

Whereas in light of
these things, Doctor Faust,

You want to be free
and free in being.

Whereas I to this
calling must comply.

In institution
of the mortal act,

We shall enter our
selves into a pact.

x.

Effective this night,
subject to the terms,

Witness before its
members this contract

Caused in part hatred,
in part discontent.

It shall be agreed
these sordid remains

Rendered heavily
to such eyes that burn.

This, like a truth
summoned, cannot be

Dismissed by conceit
or contradiction.

Without addendum,
subject to the claims,

It is yours to name,
but only in time.

Provided in good
faith, and held by trust,

This will represent
the full covenant

Between you and me,
and for the record

Superceding all
prior conventions,

Amended but by
written instrument

Signed by both parties
stating otherwise.

Consummated by
lips which pronounce it,

The force of these terms,
by powers vested,

Real or imagined
both, are eternal.

You have insisted,
it has been consigned.

Furthermore ruling
out any default,

This agreement binds
and intends to bind,

All things outside of
this notwithstanding.

In witness whereof
the parties hereto

Shall then acknowledge
the securities.

In accordance with
the order of fate

Commencing this date,
first above written,

You sign *Faust,* and I,
Mephistopheles.

Now and forever
hence the pact is made.

THE THIRD QUARTER

[XXII]

i.

It seemed but a year
ago this season,

So specific a
time, so singular

A place as here, with
the vast sky above,

And the crisp wind, the
clear night–this setting

As circumstantial
as passing weather.

ii.

And there a sly cat
inclined my fancy,

But then, as it were,
was soon forgotten

With the fleeting thought
of yet another

Frivolity: a
fallen leaf, perhaps

A child crying, or
a church bell ringing

A number no one
really cared to count.

iii.

It seemed but a year
ago this season,

So specific a
time, so singular

A moment as this,
and I was thinking

Of a woman whose
visage was not clear

In my distancing
thoughts, as such thoughts are

As circumstantial
as passing weather.

iv.

In your bounty you
defy the deities

With a greater force.
The stars once again

Align themselves to
bless the day that felled

The continuum.
Time. Space. Energy.

The kiss that collapsed
at least one heaven.

What of Valentine
were it not for us

To realize it?
We have, in effect,

Sanctified the saint.
Like music first trapped

In a soundless void,
into being brought

And made beautiful
by our sole hearing.

And it is the thought
of our next embrace

Which nurtures all that
is living in me

For another day
still, until again.

[XXIII]

i.

We met on the eve
of your departure.

We gathered at that
mansion by the lake

As the wind outside
played among the trees.

"Again the season
of autumn arrives

And the rustling leaves
rustle, submitted

To their fate. I fear
I shall not endure."

ii.

We met at the late
decline of summer

When the days had grown
short and the laughter

Of children had then
neatly subsided.

"The prospect of my
leaving I believe

Has revived me from
decay. Now, relieved,

Save what vestige will
linger in traces,

I have been thinking
of other places."

We stood together
on the balcony

And the view of the
lake that night seemed vast,

The surface of the
water reflecting

The darkness of the
trees and the clear sky.

"Just last night and to-
day, it came. And still

It comes to me as
an inflection comes.

And tonight, it will
surely come again.

You know how I feel,
more than the others.

I am delighted
that you could be here."

iii.

So we met on that
cool October eve

When leaves did flutter
outside the windows

In colors that seemed
like burnt sienna

Under the pale moon,
twilight. Prodigious,

The foliage, but
then, the night as well,

I suppose...on that
cool October eve,

The solemn eve of
your planned departure.

iv.

"So I shall leave this
place. Goodbye, at last.

Perhaps we shall not
see each other more.

With eyes closed I shall
mourn this passing fair.

But you will write me."
–I could not promise.

Trying, "I know you
can and so you must.

A few words or so
would make me happy."

–It does not seem to
have to be this way.

"I beg your pardon?"
–About your leaving.

There is nothing more
certain beyond here.

Beyond these waters,
no promise of land.

If you will permit
me Paris, Paris…

–You must forgive me.
It was a pretext.

More than the place, the
very word consumes.

"Do you ever have
thoughts of leaving this?"

–Why do you ask? "I
am not sure. Have you

Ever been in love?"
–I have lived alone.

"But certainly there
must have been a time

In your life." –There was
a woman, once. Yes.

"You loved her dearly."
–Love? I cannot say.

I should not think I
did, but then again–

You gazed into the
night and spoke to me

As the leaves outside
struggled to resist

The racing wind. "Tell
me of this woman."

–There is not much of
which to tell, really.

I searched the nights of
Paris for her face.

The nature of the
story is quite clear.

So it was, I had
returned to Paris

Charged with the feeling
that I had done well.

Then again, my thoughts,
so adolescent

In their wanderings
at that time in life,

Wanting to be with
this one or that one,

Wanting to be left,
wanting nothing more.

And then of course the
comings and goings

Of my desire to
write, desire reduced

To a mere interest,
a thought, a pattern.

This city was as
one had imagined.

It kept its promise,
lovely, to be sure

With the new glitter
on the Tour Eiffel,

Picnics on the quai,
the old bouquinistes,

Brouhaha of bars
and brawling bistros,

Around the rond-points
the racing autos

And of course, couples
kissing in the streets....

But so it was, I
walked those faubourgs

Like a man cut down
by a sharp secret

That had been withheld
for a time too long.

Having known these things
I was sure I would

Reason it all out,
if indeed reason

Were the directive.
But one thing was clear:

The next day would come
and I would awake

Just as I had done
countless times before.

I would not recall
having held those thoughts

For it seemed a time
of such forgetting.

"Will you find Paris
again soon?" –Paris?

Granted, yes, Paris
was a lovely place,

A lovely place of
young lovers. But I,

Traveling alone,
was melancholic.

v.

We met as the night
grew cold. And the wind

Like azure swings blew
through the leaves of trees

Chasing away the
laughter of children.

"You never did find
her. I am sorry."

vi.

We had met with the
gathering spirits

And spectacles as
the string quartet played

A brave counterpoint,
a close crescendo.

You extended your
hand to me, your heart

Then consumed by the
specters of your past.

"You must forgive me.
Do not be angry."

I recall now you
extended yourself

Facing the darkness
beyond window panes.

"The heart, though to its
full extent inclined,

High to the crest of
two converging waves

Cast and left without,
wanting to struggle

This precipice of
love unrequited."

The night went on its
way to afflict you

And there I was, without expectancy,

Only a desire
which I could not help.

"Suffice to have loved
and to have been loved.

Granted. What is the
measure of our lives

In the afterthought
of an emotion

Expended in vain,
spent, no longer there?"

vii.

It was then that it
came to me, standing

At the bottom of
the stairs with a plate

Of sour grapes and
cheese, waiting for you.

A moment in time
elapsed without thought,

A slow suspension
drifting as you looked.

*"Are you acquainted
with this person's work?"*

*"Many called him a
writer, but really,*

*He was a drunkard
who kept a journal.*

*I think he mostly
attended parties."*

I stood there at the
threshold with my hands

Like ice–I, being
your questionable

Escort through the dark
circles of your past.

viii.

*"Of young Icarus,
Bruegel knew nothing.*

*He hangs not at the
Musée des Beaux Arts.*

*Behold, this is how
it was, and will be...."*

*"You are the painter.
I have seen your work.*

*The faces, the hands
holding cigarettes.*

*—Curious, they are.
And intriguing, too."*

I stood and stoked the
fire with anxious hands.

I watched the flames rise
higher and higher,

Watching the rising
flames burn Icarus

Flying closer and
closer to the sun

Which was at once his
transcendence and death.

I watched these flames climb
higher and higher

All around the walls
which burned in crimson.

I watched Icarus,
Icarus on fire,

Falling down to sea
falling unconsumed

Like perpetual
falling of leaves which

Were falling outside
into the darkness

Beyond the windows.
Suddenly we kissed.

The string quartet played
a late bravado

Asserting itself
in violent bowings

As a prelude. I
cannot quite recall

But surely at some
point we must have kissed.

ix.

We met, your hand you
extended to me.

I took it, drawing
you to the terrace.

The string quartet played
in the portico

And perhaps there we
kissed, I cannot tell.

It was the eve of
your planned departure,

A cool October
eve—this much is clear.

—I know your heart is
elsewhere and not here.

And someday you will
arrive at that place.

—You must forgive me.
"I call this one 'Night

And the Circumstance.'
And this, 'Cinq Cognacs.'"

x.

We met on that eve
of your departure

With the gathering
guests, the gathering

Of plastic people
with such empty lives

Gathering around
the haute occasion,

Cocktails under the
din of rustling leaves

And the stifling daze
of conversations.

xi.

I recall the night,
frightened and sober.

The harvest moon that
stood so strong and pale

As to be severe
and the heightened wind

Like azure swings that
lashed the leaves of trees

And your failing hand
that you extended

And the string quartet
that bowed frantically

With the vengeance of
that violent tension

Sustained like a wire
tautened to a blade

And made sharp by the
moon's complicity

Were a forewarning,
a kind of prelude

To a kiss–a kiss
I cannot recall.

xii.

The dark sky, and the
wind like azure swings

With the pale moon and
the forgotten kiss

When we met on that
cool October eve,

The lonely eve of
your planned departure,

The eve of the kiss
I cannot recall.

[XXIV]

i.

Caution. So this is
what it has come to,

Doctor Faust. All these
deliberations,

All these fictitious
external factors.

The life worth living,
enlightened, explored,

With contrivances
of coffee and tea

Or false motions of
eccentricity.

Tethered to this mood,
you will think of her.

Such thoughts, classified
in *The New York Times*.

ii.

You strike a match and
light your cigarette,

Throw the burnt match stick
into the ashtray.

Inhale deeply and
contemplate the smoke

Curling blue and gray,
unfurling in space.

*The rising smoke is
not unlike that of—*

What does it matter?
Turn to the Op-Ed.

Tip the fedora,
push up the glasses.

You are distracted,
your thoughts, unwinding.

Perceiving only
your state of affairs

About which I may
be quite mistaken,

I am, however,
convinced she has more

To do with this than
I would dare to say

Or you would really
care to consider.

iii.

You have found your thin
pockets within this

Arrondissement, these
vaporous groups of

People with airs more
austere than your own.

You ruminate the
coarse calculations

And propose your own
endings in your head.

Mostly monologues
of apologies

Slipping from your speech.
This constitution,

A colloquy of
poetic non-sense

Like a stale odor
from the past, recedes.

To find transcendence
in the poverty,

The aesthetics of
the being depraved,

To negotiate
the less of it all.

The non-sequitur
to the stray tangent

Becomes eschew in
its proper vector.

iv.

It begins with a
soft sign, a moment

Thought to be lost is
retrieved by a smile.

You will incite a
conversation on

The migrant nature
of a spirit fled.

A girl across the
way closed in her book

Of nothing at all
–What are you reading?

What is it that you
dream of? Triggered by

Something misguided,
a strange governance

Of good will. *You are
sweet to ache for me,*

She would write in the
space between the lines.

v.

Out in the drizzling
restaurant terrace

A woman and a
man sit together

Shielded under a
flapping parasol.

Between them dancing
is a candlelight

Splitting the heavy
darkness as they talk.

"With you I still find
I censor my thoughts.

But perhaps one day
I will learn the words

To say, with or with-
out the poetry.

Perhaps you will be
near me to hear them."

vi.

Undecided, and
like a true skeptic

You linger, testing
its vague properties.

Incredulous though
with abated breath,

At once completely
mystified, and more,

Quite disenchanted,
a renewal of

Some obscure motion
beyond influence.

Knowing fully well,
you would do better

In the safe life of
a content bachelor.

[XXV]

i.

How shall I begin?
I had mastered this

Missive many times.
Still it eludes me.

Surely there was some
thing I had to say.

Once before in your
presence I had missed

The chance to speak up.
Now with the distance

I am no better.
Perhaps in the end

I do not have much
to relate to you.

This ineffable
thing, I have traced it

City to city
and through continents.

It ends with me not
knowing where I am.

ii.

You must excuse me
for my wanderings.

I will not worry
you with such trifles.

I should simply say
it had been lovely

In seeing you last
though both of us felt

Ill at ease at times,
each in our own way.

Forever I shall
feel undeserving

Of your attention,
much less your presence,

Entire. You must know
that I regard you

With some affection.
Our exchange last year

Au Petit remains
with me. I recall

You tried my pastis.
It reminded you

Of the sea, you said,
Méditerranée.

iii.

I think of cities,
places I have been,

I entered and left
by the double turn

Of the swinging door.
And the routes I had

Charted between them.
And people, those few

Who were once a part
of my life are now

No longer with me.
Where can they be now?

I hope you are well
and good, nonetheless.

I am writing you
from central London

Where there has been rain
or presentiment

Of rain without end.
I have been writing.

Or, might I resign,
there are the comings

And goings of my
meaningless scribblings.

I read through the lines
like a man struck down.

I shall start again.
And in so doing

I will no longer
remember these things.

I am thirty-three.
I knew I would be

One day. In the past
I had told myself

I would be elsewhere.
Here I am. *Elsewhere.*

This city is as
lonely as I thought.

[XXVI]

i.

Once again you have
taken up the pen.

Poetry, and let's
not forget Madness.

Which of the two came
first, we shall not know.

Freak twins born of the
same crippled nature.

You light another
cigarette. Inhale.

Another cup of
tea. More cigarettes.

Finding no way of
entering this world,

One thinks of the ways
of leaving. Often

One spends many nights
thinking of the ways.

Do not exclude the
possibilities.

Death by vanity,
for instance, is one.

ii.

The pause between the
clicking of the clock,

The silence between
words, between the thought

Of words, or spaces,
this lack, held tightly.

These arms will not let
go of this embrace.

*"Somewhere in all of
this, there is some good.*

*We will look back on
this sparing exchange*

*And regard it as
sacred, if not strange,*

*And deem these things worth
while. We would have to.*

*So at last, there is
beauty after all."*

iii.

This setting, perhaps
conceived for painting

With its café chairs
consigned to culture,

Fills you with desire
and melancholy.

You search out that old
photograph of her

In your head, taken
twenty years before.

She is on a train,
cradling baguettes.

Elegant and young.
A scarf thrown over

She wears light with an
affectionate touch.

Subjunctive to this
measure you summon

The yesterdays, the
many days you lost

Without requital,
neither with reason.

And with a cause quite
forgotten. Something

In your past which went
wrong. Time and again

You submitted your
self in sacrifice.

The many days in
which you stood alone,

The countless ways in
which you claimed distance.

iv.

*"You will forgive me,
yes. To be sure, I*

*Often ask for this.
You must know this much*

About me by now."
So outside the man

And the woman talk
under the constant

Shifting of the wind,
no longer shielded.

The candlelight grows
faint, and at last dies.

The late and pale moon
awakens the clouds

To converge, divide.
Converge and divide.

[XXVII]

i.

Dearest Helen—nay,
strange superlative.

Dearest for being
the only—no more.

I had a desire
to see you again.

Were it to subside,
but no, like such things

Which come in passing,
and stay all winter.

I would risk danger
of such presumption

If by chance, by fate—
whichever—you be

Inclined to lend an
ear, a moment's time

For these words, crude and
unsolicited

So to let Paris
have its way with you

Hereafter, at last,
free of my protest.

ii.

We met on the eve
of your departure,

Gathering in that
mansion by the lake

As the wind outside
played among the trees.

We met there on a
cool October eve

In the occasion
of cocktails, and there,

You extended your
self to me, your hand,

A gesture dangling
precariously

From your lithe wrist, as
if to relinquish

All to the darkness
which was to be near.

iii.

We met on the eve
of your departure

With the gathering
of guests and spirits,

Gathering of those
strangers making toasts,

The gathering for
a new beginning

To christen your plan
of travel–Paris,

The city of lights,
the city of rain.

I engaged you then
and you spoke to me

All consumed by the
darkness that was yours.

"So I shall leave this
place. Goodbye, at last.

Perhaps we shall not
see each other more."

iv.

We met on the eve
of your departure

With the gathering
of guests in that house

By the lake, and the
children dressed in white

With flowers played, run-
ning through passages,

Through promenades of
cobble stones and grass

Carelessly calling
out to their mothers.

I could but then think
of my own mother

And when I was young.
–Tell me, why Paris?

"Paris?" Your hand you
extended to me

As we half listened
to the string quartet.

There was something in
the music I heard,

The subtle cadence
of the crescendo,

The slow melody
drowning in the hall,

Entering note by
note, they played for you.

And I was happy
in your company.

v.

Sometimes things in life
get complicated.

Sometimes we forget
the simple things, like

The man, far off in
another country

Filled with wanderlust
going without sleep,

Burning down candles
listening to songs

And wishing to be
in your memory

Occasion of no
particular thing,

The weather, hot tea,
or pastis with ice.

What shall we call it,
this space in our hearts

Preemptive of that
certain otherness?

The cartography
of uncharted ways.

Vulnerable I
make myself to you,

And thereby saying
so, have done it twice.

vi.

Here and again these
hands unfold themselves,

Where I beheld with
severe scrutiny

Your tortured figure,
your elusive form

Made pale by the blue
of incandescence.

Where just to touch you
once would be enough,

To kiss your soft wrist,
to smell your wet hair.

Nothing is easy
I have learned again.

Such accursed longing–
O, such accursed rage.

Complex is fate that
twists its doubled gaze.

Something about this
is unsuspecting,

As, for instance, my
desire to write you.

It is quite beside
myself. I confess:

There is someone who
is thinking of you

Without your prior
knowledge or consent.

With no recourse I
make it known to you,

And ask your pardon
despite everything.

vii.

There can no longer
be that severance

Between the body
and the tearing soul.

The body could not
survive the vacuum,

Neither could the soul
endure the freedom.

Resolved that there is
a grave part of you

That I shall never
come to know, a part

That you will no more
reveal outwardly.

With my backward stare
of sad Orpheus,

My own vitreous
stricken white to salt

Knowing for certain
that nothing would dare

Follow my straggling
out of this Hades.

With pen and paper,
my thoughts all rabid,

Riddled by the rain
and left quite empty.

All things lead to one
end. All things, one end.

[XXVIII]

i.

Here today, before
so many choices

No longer concerned
enough to commit.

To nurture a thing.
Disposable lives

Where once beautiful
now vanish before

Averted eyes. Sworn,
such movements borrowed,

No fidelity,
none, gone tomorrow.

ii.

A scene is a scene
is a scene. This thing

We call tendency
seems a fashion which

Dictates what to be,
where to go, to do,

Or see and be seen,
stand in line waiting

For the next best thing,
a wholesale decline,

To enter the ring
for the final trial.

Walk with me a mile.
I want to hide, I

Am so terrified
of this worldliness.

iii.

What we do for such
gratification

Awaiting that thing
which will never come,

In celebration
of what is not real.

Ephemeral lives
left to compromise.

I have seen dimples
more precious than pearls,

The rarest of stones.
Spoil me with your smile.

Lavish me in your
laughter. Make me high!

Let's be seen kissing
at the fish market.

Do a shopping spree
at the bakery!

Steal me in your song.
Never let me go.

[XXIX]

i.

The evening speaks of
shadows, and the winds

Irreparable
in disposition,

Volley the glow of
the hanging lanterns.

And there you might chance
upon a feeling

Constituted of
insignificance.

And so, what of it?
This sorrow in spite

Of its own distress
with the water in

Its undulation
lapping in laughter.

The trumpets play to
the sky. This evening

Will remember the
falsetto, the jazz

As they tout out their
vertiginous cries.

All the pitiful
creatures of this earth

Transcending for a
moment into bliss.

ii.

These commodities
of moonlight and song,

Pleading insolvent
to the lost exchange

Will never afford
the happiness, the

Freedom of spirit.
Justice and beauty!

See how the light plays
on the splashing waves.

The boats lurch back and
forth without a thought,

Bound by the ritual
of their own docking.

You may watch them care-
lessly as you ask

Yourself, which part of
this landscape is real

And which is simply
an ostentation

Of an outwardly
futile projection.

iii.

There was something I
wanted to tell you.

If only I could
remember the part.

To be sure (and if
only to be sure).

Though I am not much
for words (more and more

I seem to find my
self this way) I send

This letter in the
hope that you might see.

After all, I am
a man of letters,

If I am any
thing in my essence.

iv.

All these extensions
of the useless heart

Feigning through the parts,
wishing you were here.

It means a past of
unrequitedness.

It is because I
have been infected.

And so, pensive with
portioned cigarettes

Through the slow ticking
of this endless hour.

The contours of an
emotional void

Now deeply recessed,
exceed resistance.

v.

What if one night I
conjured your image

And crossed your faint voice
over the static?

Charged by the night's rest-
less intimations.

And if I were to
deliver to you

My gross betrayal
burning like a wound?

By the wind and the
rain, I am consumed.

Far too timid for
this non occurrence,

As if lying there
for too long waiting

By the dark quarters
with the curtains drawn

In strict vigil of
that effervescence,

The forgiveness of
that unassumed act,

The final closure
for that condolence

To be made at last
quite accessible.

If I seem so, it
is because I am.

vi.

To have been born to
this world, bountiful

In its chaos and
irreverence–why?

Why not? To have peered
into the darkness

And survived its gaze.
Afraid. Unafraid.

To have wandered through
the limits of this

Mortal existence
with and without pain.

Being. Non being.
Here. And everywhere.

And still, to have found
a certain union.

Etre. Non être.
L'amour et la mort.

How full of splendor
is this? How full of–

I want to be near
you. I want to be.

vii.

I am involved by
your untold story.

And like this, without
words, you tell me how.

So I will spot you
in that dark café,

Your face lit by the
spirits as you try

And erase the years
and the false tokens.

We may write letters,
perhaps try to build

What we know to be
short of intimate–

Now impossible,
achieved but strangely.

For it may well be
maya, illusion.

[XXX]

i.

All right, all right, I
have fallen behind

In this business of
my letter writing.

Auspicious at times,
at times uninspired,

Due in part context,
in part contrivance.

Much like a poem, word
with inadequate

Word strung together,
articulating.

The sum of fragments
won't substantiate.

Little by little
it grows, then subsides.

Though so lyrical,
without gauge, its breath

Or its breathlessness.
Done in part control,

In part withholding
what is near, what is

Clearly conditioned.
What sort of new and

Wondrous event should
I recount to you?

Where shall I begin?
A matter of fact,

A matter of time,
of sequence unstrung,

A scenario
unfolding without.

ii.

Such unsuspecting
virtue from your side,

Letters of intent
to woo long distance,

An affair with a
sleight of pen in hand

Armed to deny all
of my resistance.

So having received
these various notes

Par avion, I know
I have been much less

Than reciprocal.
I will attempt then

This verse despite my
fear and the contempt

It deigns in a task
already absurd,

The indelible
meaning of these marks.

iii.

I do forgive you
for whatever wrong

You may imagine
to have committed.

As for the other,
I cannot approve

This way or that, for
it is not my place.

Can it be a crime
to think of others?

I think not. Surely
though you cannot mean

For me to be the
one of whom you think.

That desire is but
the hatred of want,

And that elusive
form of which you speak

Is only as such
—elusive. For I,

A specter of your
imagination,

The sublime thing that
needs must turn vulgar.

iv.

How shall I disguise
them? Such expressions:

I am missing you,
wishing you were here.

Pure, simple, concise
that they could not lie.

I, too, will confess
the night when we met,

The recurring eve
of my departure.

As sudden as the
failing wind that ceased,

My heart, inclined at
first, but then released.

And moonlight gathered
in the passing clouds

Were like slow shrouds of
swaddling seduction.

How could I, having
these feelings reclined,

Be accountable
for such promises

Delayed, made without
care and forsakened,

Given the night and
its circumstances

Of mitigation:
The moonlight and all.

v.

Upheld, the way un-
traversed still remains

Illuminated,
the door unopened

Still ajar. And I
have spun and unspun

My uncertainties,
holding you at bay,

And so I can no
longer decipher

What is now going,
perhaps long since gone.

The bitter after-
taste in this regret

Leaves me wretched from
its laceration.

This pain, beyond mere
words as if beyond

Mere pain, or the words
which describe this pain.

It builds in me a
wall and leaves me void.

vi.

Having surrounded
myself with sorrow

I have thoroughly
gone beside myself

This time. What was once
near and dear to me

Kept at a distance
and quickly fading.

I watch it dissolve
like snow in my hands.

Wherefore you will not
hold it against me,

That I, too, in an
affair of the flesh,

Gave myself away.
The heart and the mind,

Each better for being
their own share, and I,

Utterly alone
but for the brash night

Which advances on
my every weakness.

What remains now but
stains of misspent days

Like that last lantern
the café blows out

Whose small spark becomes
only memory

Saved in my eyes—lest
I part with nothing.

There is more, I say,
there is more, always,

Reserved as remnant
for this darkened hour

That I may posit
the constellation,

Reconstruct it as
seen by the clearest

Of April skies, star
by burning, white star.

vii.

What shall we say then
of this worn passage?

The music has changed.
The children have all

Grown up and moved on,
and I no longer

Recognize those who
were a part of me.

Still, Paris is but
a conjectured place.

I watch the pigeons
flock the old fountains

And the autumn leaves
which float like lilies

Reflecting copper
coins of wishing wells.

And I sometimes think
one could spend a life

Seeing the world move
like a downward stream,

The paradigm sun
of incandescence

Beginning its fall
into crepuscule,

And the flowers of
penury drooping

From their pots by the
broken windowpanes,

The dark clothes blown and
torn like vanquished flags.

How cruel is life that
brings us back again

To the very place
of exile and chain.

viii.

I have become tired
of so many things,

Many things with which
I used to struggle.

I no longer know
or care to learn why,

Or what, anything.
Please understand this,

The difficulty
with which I now speak,

This city and I
with everything and

Everyone with it
are never to be

Met or reconciled.
I am distant now.

ix.

My predilection
for picture postcards

And slow promenades
through cobble stone courts

May save the days of
this destitute life.

Je vous prie. I send
this faux billet doux,

Born of a heart that
is not flesh but bone,

Formed of a mind that
is laden and spent

That my heart may be
made docile, my mind

Made more light. I send
this thing with no hope,

So to say I would,
and to try, but then

To shy away and
to go on with it,

And so to let pass,
and so to live on.

[XXXI]

i.

Your letter, having
first made the journey

Via one of my
past dwellings and twice

The greater half of
three oceans, arrived

A bit belated
though not unwelcomed

And, please rest assured,
entirely intact

However well worn.
I thank you for it.

True, I did not think
I would hear from you,

Our conversation
previously having

Been perfunctory
at best, if not terse.

ii.

You will understand
that I am not so

Easy. Apropos,
I will not account

The long transcription
of my dreaded days

If only out of
shame that my days are

Composed of little,
if nothing at all.

I can say that I
have had much time to

Reflect, but also
that such reflection

Has led me back to
myself. I turn and

Turn and everything
remains quite the same.

iii.

And so in the end
my work, or non work,

Has all but become
an unimportant

Detail within this
senseless existence.

Things happen. My life
is playing itself

Out like that old dream,
familiar and strange.

Did I ever think
I could have finished?

—The poem, I mean.
I have held it now

Nearly two decades.
Still it confounds me.

Or perhaps I am
playing the role of

Fugitive after
having murdered art.

But then again I
suppose none of this

Has any bearing
on the universe.

One begins to think
reconcile, but how?

Were I some sort of
transcendentalist,

Things would be simpler.
That is to say I

Have found some kind of
loneliness, akin

To the solitude
I had known before.

I can only hope
she would recognize

This pathos and look
on with some kindness.

iv.

Cities can be cruel,
people too. Somehow

The world crowds around
us and it is this

Which gives us the sense
that we are alone.

With your permission,
I take solace in

Knowing you are near,
hoping you are well.

The pilgrimage ends
and begins again.

I shall regard you
with some affection

As we strive to find
our little places.

v.

I hurry and make
passage through the coast

Of Saint Tropez, off-
season and empty.

A glass of Sancerre
with scallops and cream,

Like a mouthful of
the white winter sea.

A remote resto,
La Bohème, provides

A tiny table
and a reading lamp.

[XXXII]

i.

"Affectations of
a Stranger," take one.

Roll film, and...action:
That morning he rose

And went to the bath-
room. He proceeded

To shave his head with
an open razor....

There is something pro-
foundly wrong with this

Picture. You have lost
the tracking device.

ii.

"Affectations of
a Stranger," take two.

Action: That morning
he awoke from sleep.

He was sweating. Bad
dreams, fever, he thought.

The cold apartment
was keen with silence.

And for a moment
the only movement

In the room was the
ceiling fan spinning.

Last night, a foregone
evening in the park,

A pointless passage
around the city,

Glitter on the Seine,
a distant siren,

A passer-by with
a trench coat and hat,

*"S'il vous plaît, monsieur,
auriez-vous une*

Cigarette?" –And cut.
He went to the bath

Room and proceeded
to shave his head with

An open razor.
He spoke out loud, "Stare

Into the mirror,
and the mirror stares

Into you...." –Full stop.
This is not working.

iii.

Begin with a scene:
A man all alone—

Or with a woman.
An apartment room.

A big city, one
oppressively dim,

Such as the one you
are presently in.

Date it back a few
years. Add some intrigue,

And some mystery.
The tension is good.

iv.

"Affectations of
a Stranger," take three.

Action: That morning
he rose out of bed.

The hot apartment
was keen with silence.

He was sweating. Bad
dreams, fever, he thought.

And for a moment
the only movement

In the room was the
ceiling fan spinning.

Cut to night table,
small clock radio,

Zoom in, 12 O'clock
blinking, cigarette

Slowly burning in
a copper ashtray,

A bowl of water.
Tilt the camera down.

A half-drunk bottle
of cheap rosé left

Corked on the floor by
the bed. A blood-stained

Shirt curls around it.
Dissolve black and white:

Last night, a foregone
outing on the île,

A directionless
walk over a bridge,

Glitter on the Seine,
a distant church bell,

A passer-by with
a t-shirt and cap,

*"Excuse-moi, t'as pas
une cigarette?"* –Non.

And everywhere, heat
and incandescence

Of a Parisian
evening in late June.

v.

He put his hand in
the bowl of water

And wiped his face. He
let out a deep breath.

He stood up and moved
to the small window,

Drawing the curtain.
He let the late sun

Fall on his cheek. He
lit a cigarette

And looked out to the
market on the street.

What is to be done?
–Nothing to be done.

The revolution
was over and won.

There was nothing left.
No more cause-effect.

He looked at his hands.
Dissolve, black and white.

Disrupt vertical
hold. Dissolve, color.

The man moved to the
window and looked out.

The noise from the fish-
market was fading.

Slow pan of camera
to the street. Close in:

A child holding on
to his mother's arm.

The man spoke softly,
"The traffic is like

An orchestra, no?"
–Such meaninglessness.

Then it came to him,
and quite suddenly:

He never knew her,
nor did she know him.

Once contented in
being alone, now,

All was lost. –Cut. He
went to the bathroom,

Turned the sink faucet
on with a loud squeak.

He lowered his head
under the cold stream

And let the water
run down through his hair.

In slow motion: He
lifts his head, water

Streaming down his face.
Voice over, the man

Humming an old jazz
tune. He then proceeds

To shave his head with
an open razor.

Burn to white, the bath-
room floor: Clumps of hair

In slow motion fall
to the white, tile floor.

Over-exposure:
Clumps of hair falling

Continuously,
fading into white.

Motionless, the frame
frozen on the floor.

Slow dissolve to the
man: Now without hair

Razor in hand, "Stare
into the mirror

And the mirror stares
into you. How true."

vi.

"Affectations..." roll
black and white. Take four,

Action. Camera close-
up of night table:

The clock ticking past
twelve, a cigarette

Slowly burning in
a silver ashtray,

A bowl of water.
The hot apartment

Is keen with silence.
Tilt the camera down:

A bottle of red
half-drunken and left

Corked on the floor by
the bed. A stained shirt

Curls around it. The
man, awake, sits up.

He is sweating. Bad
dreams, fever, he thinks.

vii.

"What is your name?" "–I
am not to tell you."

"You won't tell me. What
shall I then call you?"

"–You need not call me.
Here is the package.

Further instructions
to follow shortly."

"Will you stay a bit?"
"–I am to leave now."

Disrupt vertical
hold, bleed red, and cut.

viii.

The sunrise is late.
The room is washed grey.

The woman, sleeping,
her body naked

To the heat, glowing
pale in the background.

And for a moment
the only movement

In the room is the
stream of smoke rising.

He puts his hand in
the bowl of water

And wipes his face. He
lets out a deep breath.

He stands up and moves
to the small window,

Draws up the curtain
letting the new sun

Fall on his cheek. He
lights a cigarette

And looks out to the
market on the street.

A small spider falls
to the window sill

And begins to crawl
across unnoticed.

"What is to be done?
Nothing to be done."

There is nothing left,
no affectations.

He looks at his hands,
hands which learn, but then

Quickly forget. The
hands which must relearn.

ix.

Suddenly the day
apprehends the room.

The woman, lying
blurred in the background,

Prostrate then fetal,
disquietly shifts.

She wets her dry lips.
She opens her eyes

Slowly. A quiver.
She turns to watch him

Quietly as he
smokes by the window.

"Would that this love like
a prayer ascend

And be heard.... No, not
in this life. It can't."

The man turns to see
the woman awake.

"The heart and the mind,
two sons of one god

Driven against each
other, given knives

And together cast
into an abyss."

Her eyes slowly fall
closed. –Dissolve to white.

x.

The sound from the fruit
vendor dissipates.

Wide pan of camera
to the street, close in:

A boy holding on
to his mother's arm.

Camera pulls back through
the window, tilts down:

The man sees the small
spider by his hand.

He watches it for
a moment blankly,

Says to it softly,
"The traffic outside

Is an orchestra."
He extinguishes

The slow cigarette
over the spider.

A snuffed trail of smoke
dances through his hand.

He raises his head
with eyes closed and turns....

Once contented in
being alive, but now,

All is lost. –Cut. He
goes to the bathroom,

Turns the sink faucet
on with a shrill sound.

He lowers his head
to the cold water

And lets the water
run down through his hair.

And under the rush
of the stream he hears

Only the leaking
pipe's crystalline drip

Shallowed to puddles,
reverberating

In a dark basement
cellar he once knew,

Unforgotten of
his childhood recluse.

xi.

Slow motion: He lifts
his head, the water

Streaming down his face.
Voice over, the man

Begins to hum to
himself low, *"How strange*

*The change from major
to minor...."* He starts

To shave his head with
an open razor.

Burn to white, the bath-
room floor: Clumps of hair

In slow motion fall
to the white, tile floor.

Gradual over-
exposure: More clumps

Of hair continue
the staggered falling.

Slow dissolve to the
man: Now without hair,

Razor in hand, blood
streaking down his face.

Filter in red. "Stare
into the mirror

And the mirror stares
into you. How true."

xii.

She is sleeping on
the floor with her shirt

Unbuttoned by heat,
her hair disheveled.

Cautiously the sun
comes into the room.

She lays there, moves from
prostrate to fetal.

She wets her dry lips
and, with a quiver,

She opens her eyes.
She watches his form

By the window smok-
ing a cigarette.

"Perhaps for a time
you had loved that child,

And perhaps you still
do. And possibly

Your love like a prayer
will ascend somewhere

And be heard. But not
in this life. It can't."

The man turns to see
the woman awake.

"I have been asking
myself if we shall

See each other more
and that if we do,

In which circumstance
we would meet, whether

Extended or brief,
intimate or no."

Burn to white, dissolve.
"You have gathered your

Things. You have put on
an air of leaving...

And leave, so only
my cigarette smoke

Follows you out the
door. But all else is

Not motionless in
this room made sordid

By your departure.
For instance my heart

Which stirs like a stone
on the precipice

Made precarious
by the gods and I,

Like Sisyphus, must
once again struggle.

How could I have known
about the blind steed

Saddled, galloping,
fervent in its stall?

Like a temple with
passage forbidden,

You, affectedly
dark with mystery."

Her eyes slowly close.
—Burn to white. Dissolve.

"We should have known, life
is so suspecting,

Unsuspectingly."
—Slow dissolve to black.

xiii.

"Between life and love
I have chosen death.

By all that is good,
I have lost my way.

I shall not know now
the joy which follows

Or does not follow.
It must be this way.

Love, supposedly
blind, is in the end

Discerning. It is
patient, but only

For a time. It is
above all, anxious.

Irreverent and full
of expectancy.

Often forgetful,
seldom forgiving.

And what mystery
beyond this sorrow

Inexplicable?
We give and give, but

Then we borrow back
in equal measure.

True we had loved much,
but perhaps not well.

We are both of us
guilty of a sin

Which can never be."
—Burn to black. Dissolve.

xiv.

"Affectations of
a Stranger." Take five,

Action: That morning
he rose out of bed.

He went to the bath-
room for the razor

And proceeded to
calmly shave his head.

[XXXIII]

i.

Of the waning in
autumn's space and time,

And of pain, and of
the withering bloom,

Of the dissonance
in the weathered wings,

Or of distancing
things in breathless swoons,

And of all such days
of upset frailties,

None more distraught than
of these declining,

Dissipated leaves.
What did it matter

That the bough once cast
brisk and tenantless

Against the coldest
night came back in bloom?

As it was born, it
died—was then reborn

To die again so
carelessly, alas,

Without certainty
in silence always

Against the countless
seasons which expire.

ii.

Journey again by
the crowning of clouds,

Higher and higher
through the wayward paths

Of rustling leaves and
of deceiving tracks

Directed only
by the shafts of light

Quivering of smoke
rising. All to see

The foliage and
feel the mountain wind.

iii.

It is heard and seen
spreading far beyond

Plains of poverty
and the barren slopes

Of yellow and of
green half-tended hopes

Where the farmers with
sharpened plows struggled

And the lone sower,
now two seasons past,

Despite the shadows
of trailing black birds,

Descended the fields
with a sack shouldered

Casting the seeds out
to the wind with faith,

And futility.
The blades which sifted

The stubborn soil, now
without cause and dulled,

Tarnish upended
in the empty barns.

What can portend this
more clearly? A sight

Which speaks nothing of
love or motherhood.

Something in this fore-
boding strains the blood,

With this land like a
body of water

One can scarcely stir
with a pebble thrown.

iv.

Hear the derisive
laughter of the wind

Against the leaves of
trees, the heedless rain

Knocking against the
broken house, the storm

Mocking in horror
over the ruins.

See the wretched walls,
smashed, or decomposed.

Listen, the wailing
calls which still resound

Through the carcasses
of rubble and dust,

The steel colored and
corroded with rust,

Bleeding in decay,
the slowly dying,

And the dead. Picture
the grand exodus,

Fleeing from the plight
in decrepit herds

Of prey. You can hear
the distancing din

Echoing fervent
throughout the valley.

v.

Where the faggot burned
the last central fire

The black patch of stone
and dirt, there becomes

The myth and legend.
So the hallowed ground

The pillars of fire
scorched, where paladins

Were kept from yeomen
fled and miracle

Did occur. Here, the
sunken chariots

In the mud and reeds.
And there, the reinless

Steeds caught and drowned in
the converging waves.

It was the livestock
left behind in haste,

The cargo, fallen.
Throughout this wasteland,

The venerable
creek flooded over

By the watershed
and the broken mill,

Chimeras shake the
graves of romantics,

Awakening the
souls once forgotten.

vi.

Here, you had pitched your
tent and gathered wood

To kindle aflame
the darkening earth.

You withdrew the stick
of burning ember

Out of the fire to
pierce the frozen night

And so to invoke
the dancer and the

Muse to leap and sing
in recitation.

Fugitive as these
words, like a blanket

Unfurled, the story
expires with the dawn

And escapes the mind
in sleep. The embers

Of the exhausting
fire heave its last great

Glittering breath. The
glow grows dim and dies,

The earth's horizon
with emerging light

Becomes keener in
your obscuring eyes.

vii.

You who have no pre-
emptive claim on dawn

Rise to the light that
charges your chilled blood.

Surely now your rent
flesh has come to know

After years of pain
well contemplated,

This awakening
is but the learning

Of a leitmotif,
never to follow,

Paused so to begin
all over again.

Alas, as it is
born, it dies—is then

Reborn again to
die so senselessly.

What transformation
is then lived, useless

But one returning
to your life to face

Yourself again in
the fading darkness

And the cold? You wake
to the morning chill,

The extinguished fire,
the fields wet with dew.

[XXXIV]

i.

Crystal flakes shudder
still in their waking.

Spotted lights begin
to fall through dim eyes.

The old hand under
a shadow breaking

Discovers itself
in darkness again,

Stark of another
hand now departed,

Where days let go of
recalling the strain

Arrive at little.
What but a vestige,

That verse retreating
in a staggered tear

Like sonnets hidden
in a dresser drawer,

Recessed nostalgia
in the black cashmere.

ii.

In sorrow of days
spent of soul and self

From the wealth of a
terrifying grace

I count the absence,
the tolling of hours,

In the library,
the empty parlor,

In the many rooms
where canvases hang,

Strict variations
of all the embraced

Lovers despairing
of the coming end.

THE FOURTH QUARTER

[XXXV]

i.

Serendipitous
the soprano sings.

A tiny act on
a tiny stage, red

With velvet curtains.
The magician's wand

Waves plastic circles.
The ruffled paper

Flowers spring from wires.
The harlequin with

Reptilian grace
strews the kerchiefs, one

After another,
so softly falling

Like the uncertain
sentiment that's mine.

ii.

An outdoor café,
a cooler candor,

But free of any
interpolation.

Faust, Wagner, seated
over a chessboard.

A stick of incense
slowly burns itself.

Mephistopheles
lurks in the background

Unnoticed, peering
over their shoulders.

iii.

The maker makes the
motions, we comply.

The chooser chooses
choices then denies

The human component,
programmed to fail.

So the held hand of
a marionette

Shifts its static smile
slightly in its box.

iv.

You turn, you counter-
turn, but shall not stand.

Michael has fallen
into the embrace

Of his destroyer.
Do not be deceived,

There is strophe and then
there is anti-strophe,

But now the tongue of
epode is severed.

There is argument
without a body,

Prelude without song,
and introduction

Leads not text like a
portico that ends.

In prologue somewhere
on earth or heaven,

Counterpoint voices
in grave dissonance

Chant wavering without resolution.

The angels perform
a simple ballad,

"Refusal to Mourn
the Death of Michael."

v.

*Were it not for you
standing there looking*

*The finer of both
halves, unreconciled*

*But not broken in
the strength of your will.*

*And were it not for
your treacherous ways.*

*The mind is split in
to want and wanting.*

vi.

I would not have come
here so soon if not

In fear of missing
your goodbye, and so

It is I arrived
to sit with my tea

A bit by your side,
watch the birds, perhaps

Play a game of chess.
Could be the nicest

Way to spend the day.
—Black or white, Doctor?

No respite it seems,
the difficulty

In speech, and I, a
supposed poet.

How should I tell, how
should I tell, indeed?

*Tell it in style, tell
it in whole. —Attack!*

Defend—would that this
rhyme be so simple.

*Formidable with
the Sicilian!*

You will not believe
the tale which follows.

What resolution
creating conflict—

Strange, the light that wanes
with the water's flow.

And where pain secedes
there is succession

of but greater pain.
Slow revolution.

vii.

At the start of the
century was war.

Push a pawn. Last night,
a long promenade.

In the rain? What for?
Not for much, really.

And so, what happened?
Nothing. The rain fell.

Intently. So in-
tently did the rain

Fall on the commons
as I walked. I walked

For hours in that rain,
and nothing happened.

So poetic was
its serene display.

So murmurous its
calm oblivion.

But understand this,
nothing will happen.

Nothing would happen
in such stagnation.

You castle. Push a
pawn. *En passant, yes.*

The downpour had ceased
and I walked further.

Through the pergola
passages winding

With wild ivy in
exposed gardens lined

By flowers, I saw
next to the brushes,

A child's red wagon
filled with rain-water,

Abandoned to the
storm the night before,

Its front wheels tilted
in late urgency.

The first of morning
birds perched at its edge

And drank from its pool,
unwitting, careless.

viii.

*Shortly after the
war, there was war still.*

We met over tea
and realpolitik.

Some things, in search of
opportunity,

Cannot be denied.
At the next table,

A struggle of chess
in certain impasse:

No side recalled whose
turn it really was

And all the pieces
were quite gray. You kept

Looking as if you
knew a better move.

Counting the sparrows
dead along the way

I realized that the
balance of the day

Had been disrupted,
the harmony, now

Beyond any hope
of reparation.

Thus did the dark hours
pass. Nothing happened.

–You check me, Wagner?
I know you, Doctor,

*Though not too well, well
enough to accord.*

*Over triumph and
tragedy you closed*

*The ring which hinged the
fated alliance.*

*With equal parts of
mistrust and fearing*

*You sealed our greatest
moment of revolt.*

We turn the wheel–in
what unifying

Dizziness it turns.
Breathless begins the

Resuscitation.
The meaningless thoughts

Of an ill mind form
in such weariness.

ix.

May, may not–the first
of tautologies.

Nay, perhaps not. *L'homme
est né libre, mais—*

Forever he is
in chains. Truth, followed

By a truism.
Always, truism

Follows truth. *—That, too,
is a truism.*

There is such a thing
as fear, now I know.

This, then, will be my
final parable.

x.

*Yes, our finest hour
indeed, however*

*Ambiguous in
its Enigmatic*

*Elements. Have you
forgotten the scene,*

*In old Coventry,
year 1940,*

*Moonlight Sonata
playing overhead,*

*And the glorious
fireworks above us.*

*The gathering storm
had filled six buckets*

*Through each aperture
in the parasol*

*As your face swayed from
dead-pan to laughter,*

*Dead-pan to laughter,
and then back again.*

xi.

*You have survived long
nights thinking of death*

*And of dying, and
of the lifelessness*

*In its resistance,
turning you to stone.*

*You have observed how
the heart and the mind*

*In successive steps
combat and descend*

*Into the obscure
blindness of all thoughts.*

*Freedom is not with-
out its price, Doctor.*

*—But not quite enough
cold water to quench*

*Those few—some here, some
there—unfortunate,*

*Being at the wrong
time and the wrong place,*

*Upon whom the night
of barbarism*

*Descended uncut
by the restless stars.*

*You stood at the watch-
tower in defense*

*Of that sacrifice,
of that which was doomed.*

*Another stony
path that we may tread.*

*Not one precious word
of warning whispered.*

*Not one visible
torch silently lit.*

*The Enigma so
overly sustained,*

*This precarious
vibrato carried*

*Much like a certain
other sonata*

*I was thinking of
known by the same name.*

*Diminutive in
your disguise, your part,*

*The ritual of
abstinence, you start.*

*It is a matter
of strict reduction.*

*Mise-en-scène to this
irrelevant act,*

*The dramatic cue
without Personae.*

xii.

*In new Coventry,
Cathedral rebuilt,*

*On the eastern side
the sun would arise*

*Against St. Michael
and the old devil.*

*Benevolence, that
God-forsaken word,*

*Means nothing in the
face of compassion.*

*More scarce than justice
is this compassion.*

*With satan reclined
in his submission*

*Saint Michael showed this
being his ration.*

xiii.

We are left ill to
our own devices

And the vastness of
that indifference.

*I, hating every
motif of your most*

*Grandiose gestures,
always as they were*

*Wont to command some
thing and anything.*

*Your red cheeks smiling
so stupidly then,*

*Your cigar burning
slowly like a stump*

*And the stench of its
smoke thickly climbing*

*The parasol post.
See how I, too, stride*

*Up the steps of the
viceregal palace*

*Half naked with my
worthless sedition.*

*But all I wanted
really was to steal*

*A glance from the child
faint with his mother.*

I fear that this night
will turn me to stone

And by my own weight
be stricken to sand.

*A slow death indeed
—Check. Doctor, beware.*

It is not easy
to have lived through both.

*That's what you said the
last time as you bore*

*The buckets to claim
your consolation*

*—Another lie in
which to line your guise,*

*Divided, at last,
to ashes, to dust.*

*A veritable
coup! —Check, no defense.*

Sometimes you have to
sacrifice the queen.

*With impunity?
—Check again, Doctor.*

So gather the bricks,
churn the new mortar.

So place them one on
top of the other.

xiv.

On the tallest hill
which the sovereign sun

Strikes first at dawn, stands
a desolate tree

Where pushes strident
a curious bough.

To where contending
element and time

A bird will fly to
build a nest of pomp.

*Check again, Doctor
—Mate! Your castle sacked,*

*The glass wall shattered
before the third act,*

*Disbelief like a
black curtain suspends,*

*This tragedy played
out without respite,*

*And recognition
far beyond recall.*

*Thy city fallen,
full fathom, descends.*

Let the water shape
the rocks, there is time.

*Where now, tell me, is
the strong one, Doctor?*

Swords have clashed, cities
torched down to embers,

Men dragged witless like
cinders through the fire.

Time wounds then, as does
space, and my tongue turns

At the aftertaste
of words affected.

xv.

The inadequate
paltry littering

Through the longest nights
in the secret hours

Of thieves and lovers'
sleep now brought to close.

The herd rounded home
despite the fled sheep–

The fled sheep cares not,
indeed, would rather

Wander than be skinned.
Never performed, how

Shall it endeavor
rendered thoroughly

In self-effacement
and dissipation?

Staged but in the mind
what measures destined

But those meager and
ineffectual?

Disregarded plates
of antiquity

Have been scattered clean,
one by one to the

Very last, shattered.
Only shards remain.

Undone by our own,
we have delved deeper

Into the sorrow
unequivocal.

So humanity
lies prostrate on fields

Of its forlorn. Fear
and hate tightly weave

To tether the soul.
O, disillusion!

The very word drives
song birds of desire

To flee the boughs of
eternal season.

xvi.

All that is divine
snakes through the labyrinth

Of mortal device,
so divinity

Will escape the self.
The mortar and the

Crucible, if not
the dark sepulcher,

The very chambers
of our own construct,

To crush and burn, to
churn and separate,

To dissipate, and
at last, to take from

The bridge the stones and
reassemble them

To form the alter
and the prison wall.

Unretrieved anchors
rest on ocean floors

As tattered sails shift
the winds at half-staff.

Distant bells toll the
wake like pendulums

Resounding in depths
of disquiet dreams.

The chorus of
angels in the end,

Of Gabriel and
Raphael, shall chant

In deaf dissonance
wavering until

We sleep, motionless
with indifference,

Divided, fatigued.
What measures destined

But those fettered
and infecund? No,

Let it stand. Let it
stand, whether to be

Laid down or held high
in exaltation.

Let be. Indeed, let
be the way it was.

[XXXVI]

i.

Nothing left of this
mystic legacy

But the stale legend
and the depictions

By the Old Masters.
The crucifixion

And the dry descent,
the Pietà and

The deposition,
electrifying

The sole sacrifice,
the pale ecstasy

Thus edifying
this strict sanctity.

ii.

Let it be known: that
which is raised will fall

With force, what is wrought
only dashed apart.

And he that God him-
self made flesh foresaw,

Driven by the pain
and the poverty

Of a people, with
hate and fear carried

In panniers, a cross
of infinite weight.

iii.

From Pontius to
Magi search, but find

Neither miracle
nor resurrection,

No hands bearing the
living stigmata.

I.e., the great stone
stands in place unmoved.

Gaze with solemn eyes
but witness no claim.

Whose will was it, this
immutable pain?

iv.

The rebel and the
self-immolator,

The fatalistic
fakir and the fool,

Those despairing by
the desolate shores

Will thus proclaim the
death of their maker.

The litany of
protest unanswered

Will burn, unseen, and
so fiercer for it.

v.

Struggle is the one
ascending mountains.

He is the exiled
native returned home.

He is the charter
lost, a pilgrimage

Without vision of
that which is sacred,

The horsemen on a
starless, flightless night.

You who are among
the lesser inclined,

The last, stunned specter
of this endless and

Uncertain waking,
proceed in a daze.

Yours is a totem
face chiseled in stone,

So harshly sun scorched
and so rain beaten.

vi.

*I sought beauty in
the cathedral ruins*

*In the tragic site
of a holy fire,*

*Under marble blocks
smashed by heaven's ire*

*Where solemn remains
of blackened piles marked*

*Pavilions which once
housed a pantheon*

*Of gods, where pillars
of a colonnade*

*Once stood proud like the
people and divine.*

vii.

*I sought beauty in
the stern aftermath*

*Of devastation
and apocalypse.*

*Church and monument,
tower and palace,*

*A city laid waste
alongside Babel,*

*Constructed stone and
steel asunder dashed,*

*Civilization's
sanctioned slab and slate*

Shattered by the inexorable weight.

*This city fallen,
its culture muted*

*And marred, ravaged were
the worthless treasures,*

*Tangled, broken, strewn
the icons burlesque.*

*What meaningless spoils
there did I behold?*

*—So little left to
tell of holiness.*

*Those splintered glimpses
into staggered eyes,*

*The scattered litter
so complete. I asked,*

*Will the parts, this time,
make the whole? Perhaps.*

*In waking to dream
I saw what might be*

*In that which seemed the
final being. I knew*

*In the end, a part
of this, and a part*

*Of myself could not
perish, in the end.*

[XXXVII]

i.

To go on in the
absence of desire–

Shall we consider
the alternatives?

The despairing one,
the one with his face

Folded in his hands,
the one who can't speak.

Hope it was worth while.
–*Be reasonable.*

He would be in need
of love, not reason.

–The lack of which is
simply a meaning-

Less consequence of
lacking the former.

The eyes defile the
mind. The mind in stride

Defiles the spirit.
Better lose the eyes

Lest we then be barred
from heaven above.

ii.

Suppose I go through
the random motions

And assume the acts
in isolation,

This one, then that one,
to live out the days

In banalities.
Neither here nor there.

It leads to a time
overwhelmed. The hand

Will unfurl itself
and release the ring.

I will speak the line,
it cannot be so.

In my beginning
is my solemn end.

Because I have paused
I shall pause again.

iii.

Suppose I sat here
for hours without thought

Like a book of poems
placed on a table

–And so I have. And
if I were to sit

Here without a sound
in this asylum

Without suffrage? But
alas, and I have.

The bane hour lives on
without words, without

A word. Listless the
yearning, motionless

Each extension, and
breathless every sigh.

All that we are, all
that we claim to be,

All that we devise,
annexed of our being,

This ineffable
rebus of disdain,

Believing nothing
outside of ourselves

Much like the caustic
inquiry of *why*,

Rhymed, now reasoned, will
signify little.

The recitation
"Give us this day" will

Make anterior
our starved existence.

iv.

Too late now to be
lamenting that loss,

The nostalgia for
that defeated hour

So curious in
its imperfection.

All is negation,
I can see this now,

Disintegral in
our understanding.

You propose the phrase,
you can never find

The same beauty twice,
and hear the reply,

You cannot find that
beauty even once.

v.

Supposing it has
truly come to this,

This evening full of
wonder and sadness,

This fitful constant
found of conjecture.

Or, supposing this
movement does not end.

It has been a thought
of mine for some time.

The finite feeling
in a disrupt grace,

The late tendencies
of a backward gaze,

The posthumous and
sustainable sigh,

The prophetic twitch,
the conjugal touch.

So I start again.
I trace the scripting

Of the page, a scar.
I transcribe the text,

What is true now will
be so forever.

In my beginning
is also my end.

Because I have sung,
I shall sing again.

My prayers fall as
they release their sounds.

vi.

The plaintiff gestures
of an infirm hand

In the acting out
of novice notions,

To go on in the
absence of angels,

In the absence of
the very longing,

–This night, unlikely
to service the need.

So I roll one last
cigarette and place

It on the table.
Pour the hot water

And watch the steam rise.
I wait the length of

The night until I
can wait no longer.

What should one surmise?
–A tale worth telling

In memoriam
of one's flesh and soul,

Unwaning of one's
deepest sentiments.

[XXXVIII]

i.

An abstraction of
a near rudiment

With an idea
hypothetical

Takes shape without form.
A metaphor of

An outer motion
is inwardly shown.

A semblance in the
sense of the subject

Half submerged in an
uncertain feeling

Hints at the signals.
But only hinting.

A glimmer here, a
shadow there. Beyond

The dark a vestige
of an old fragment

Lies unassuming.
What do these things mean?

The kinetics of
possibility

Are unshaken by
probability.

ii.

There is no mystery
to be discovered,

Save the unwilling-
ness to be present.

The mythology
of the new rite is

The same old passage.
The same old, same old.

We should be wise to
let them go, and be

Made wiser for the
letting go of them.

iii.

It happens like this:
A man sits at his

Desk, takes off his shoes.
Then everything ends.

The mind's formation
of disturbances

Flashes out warnings
in a tortured font,

Units of decay
post-scripting errors.

A containment too
fatal to release,

The unnatural
order of these things,

Paradigms that close
with impounding force,

The human valence
reduced to zero,

The twisted helix
itself uprooted.

Virtually absent
in the virtual

Realities of
an assaulting glare,

A twitching finger
clicking to obtain

Senseless artifacts,
downloadable lives.

Abstract engines search
the conjectured void.

In waves, in particles
the meters run red.

The sensors distort
the signal warning.

The synapse conducts
the cancerous pulse.

I cannot impose
on this patron saint.

The lone flame fatigued
in the frozen night,

So cold it does not
move. It simply burns.

iv.

With God's hour ended
the angels depart

One by one in a
chorus of fleeing.

Fight this sharp longing,
another longing

Ad infinitum
of what is absurd

Under a grace that
never parts and is,

Despite itself, cruel
in its unending.

v.

Over and again
the stiff mantra scores

The ultimate loss.
Irreversible

Missingness. Space carved
of a thing let go.

Nothing will fill it.
Empty it shall rest.

The disturbances
ripple in the sand.

The closed circular
meditation stands.

The needles form the
matrix that informs.

God, no God. But God
nonetheless, in whole.

vi.

There is no center.
The sphere extends not.

The circumspection
of thought unravels.

For what triumph of
idolatry will,

Deigns not to move the
smallest of the stones.

Order undone. No
faith will restore it.

I shall not believe
for it is not true.

[XXXIX]

i.

Why in the solemn
night when the cool rain

Will make its sound, light
on the window panes

Or light against the
leaves of trees, or there,

Deep against the dark,
do our hearts quiver

Like a shivering
child wild with fever?

ii.

Walls intermingle
leather bound and brick,

Partitions ardent
with crystalline chords,

Impasse high, this time
without any choir.

The weight of hundreds
of years and beyond

Without forgiveness,
without much giving.

iii.

So much seen though so
little understood.

Elusive things sought,
distraught ways followed,

Though many seasons
have come unnoticed,

The taller questions
linger unanswered.

Still they survive the
strange passing of time,

This strangeness which will
endure beyond death.

iv.

Older and more wise
these hands first remove

The stiff spectacles
to place them aside.

Then with palms pressed in
to eyes, a deep sigh.

Then follows the look
stricken, bewildered

By the years that seem
to pass unfurnished.

A near thought in its
forming dissipates.

Now for the real trial,
let's play it again.

The stunned hands failing
their desperate grasp,

A book let go, falls
closed in a corner.

v.

So these things, here and
there, are but like dust.

They do not define
the object standing

By the dying fire.
So it is, alas,

I do not ask, how
do you spend your days?

Do your surroundings
suit you well enough?

Rather I should ask,
how deep do you hurt?

How heavy is your
loneliness? Or this:

How soon from now does
your despair impend?

*Our lives spent in search
of that sacred place,*

*Swimming upstream to
our burial ground.*

*We submit ourselves
already emptied*

*Of our spirit we
lost along the way.*

A primal panic
thus postulated,

This will pass. This, too,
will pass, as all things

In respective turn.
But still, any task

Beyond the muted
culture of coffee

And cigarettes seems
quite astonishing.

vi.

The closer, the more
distorted, your thoughts,

Relativity
of the cognitive.

Initiative in
keeping with Newton:

A subject at rest
will remain at rest.

That hesitation
without circumference

Whose center is found
everywhere at once

Is yet with half the
distance remaining.

Ambition is that
arrow suspended

In flight. Pioneer
or revisionist

Lost in history's
strange contingencies.

vii.

All these years you sat,
legs crossed in repose,

A volatile mass
without energy,

Peering through those bent
glasses tuned to pitch.

Four and twenty years
and what happens now?

At last, frost descends
upon the sparrow,

Sparrow for sparrow.
–Quid pro quo, Doctor.

It had been agreed.
Deliver, you must.

Turn to the darkness
and the cold. See how

The trees relinquish
accepting sorrow.

You, like the leaves, though
so boisterous, so frail

In motion, short of
intrepid, submit

To the wind, never
to rise up again.

POSTLUDE

[XL]

i.

Perhaps the story
has played itself out.

After all, the grand
finale had its

Finality there-
in contained, and what

Seemed to be in the
end was all there was.

ii.

I have been here for
what feels forever

Toying with matches
and the irony.

It is needed for
something, I suspect.

Three days straight, no breaks,
only cigarettes.

No impunity
in this self-pity.

How much longer now?
And the lungs fight back.

Fear of dying is
like this, I am told.

Inhabiting an
uninspired space,

Walking room to room
with no memory,

Growing old, sitting
and waiting for soon.

We have witnessed this
before, the frontiers

Beyond whose lines one
can know nothing more.

iii.

The trees outside have
lost their foliage.

We fall back on the
clocks an hour late.

I shall remember
on a later date,

This recurrence of
eternal season,

This diminishing
return of reason.

The time and the age,
far from perfection,

Destiny and rage
in this denouement

Of unrelent. So
the body now rent,

A cadaver flanked,
blood of disbelief.

And outside a leaf
falls. A falling leaf–

What does this really
mean? I do not think

They will hear my speech
to the very end.

iv.

I understand it
to be the purpose

Of an unseen hand,
its contrivances.

Intent is for eyes.
Motive, for fingers.

We are the puppets
of contingency.

The frayed sutures of
our divided will—

Yes and yes, or no—
as each stitch informs

The binary code
of our discontent.

v.

I trace the makings
of the page, the scars.

I recite the words
(again, the same words)

In my final end
is my beginning.

Because I have turned
I shall turn again.

For in my coming
I have gone too far,

In departing I
have at last arrived.

vi.

What is fair, what is
foul, time will assign.

Unwittingly we
wash our hands with blood.

Whereof we flee, there-
of fate awaits us,

And, as such, always
by date appointed.

Pierced by the quick of
a thousand arrows,

There are no more ears
for incantations.

Volatile, your heart
I have seen withstand

Pain immutable
even by prayer.

Poet, logician
priest and martyr–all,

Indentured servants
to distance and time

Against the garden,
elusive, wherein

Entrance is the first
disobedience,

Rise now and turn back,
conjecture nothing

From this wasted scene,
divided in vain.

For the little that
is, and the little

That will be, this you
will not understand.

vii.

You may nest these nights
in writing letters,

Your hand flickering
beside candle lights

With deep and heavy
incense lit, its smoke

Exuding in streams
climbing into dark.

You may shed tears to
this melancholy.

You may walk these sleep-
less nights, or simply

Dream of walking these
nights so sleeplessly

By the restless shores
of recollection,

Biding metaphors
with care and patience,

Awaiting the lost
past to be absolved

And delivered whole
with the sun's advent

Or in shimmers on
the recurring waves

Which roll and tumble
and extend too soon,

Only to expire
again at your feet.

So it shall be said,
here lies half a man,

His constitution
made only in part.

His faint memories
scattered to nothing.

APPENDIX

APPENDIX

From
CITIES & DUST

New York,

How shall I begin? I have marveled at this missive many times and still it eludes me. Surely there was something I wanted to say. So many times in your presence I had missed the occasion to speak. And still with the distance I am no better. Perhaps in the end, I do not have much to convey.

This ineffable thing...I have traced it, city to city and through continents. It ends with me not knowing where I am.

You must excuse me for my wanderings. I should not worry you with such preoccupations. I should simply say it was lovely to hear your voice when we last spoke, even if our meeting was only brief.

Forever I shall feel undeserving of your attention, much less your presence, entire. You must realize by now that I regard you with some affection. Our exchange last year at the café remains with me. I recall you had sipped my pastis saying it reminded you of the Mediterranean.

I think of cities...cities I had entered, entered and left by the double swing of the gate's pendulum. And the routes I had charted between them. And people, people who were once a part of my life but are no longer. Where are they now?

Yes, I have been writing, since you ask. I am looking toward completing another edition of the manuscript. It will be five years this winter – about the time we have known each other. Much is still a mystery.

So it is our lives have taken different turns. Perhaps we are destined to write each other like this, and only propose to one another such visitations. Still, I hope to remain in contact, even if only sparingly.

Please send your new address when you make your move. I will look forward to speaking with you more.

Paris

Minneapolis,

I received the package, thank you. I apologize for the frequent and importune requests coming from my end. You did not realize you would be the guardian of my worthless estate during my travels. I hope you are well nonetheless.

I am writing you from London where there has been rain, or the presentiment of rain, for the past two weeks. I am reminded once again that this kingdom, however united, is having a serious problem with taking care of its youth. Just in the course of the opening of this letter which I am writing from a restaurant terrace, I have witnessed several transient adolescents, sleeping bags slung over shoulders, asking for spare change.

Meanwhile, London continues to rank as the greatest of European destinations, and claims itself as one of the most desired places to live. My mind, however, lacking the essential imagination, is incapable of making this leap. Notwithstanding the stench of royalty, this city remains insistently mediocre much like many other cities with its littered walks described in some Elliot poem.

Sorry if this news is disenchanting to you – you who must be looking on to this island for a kind of salvation. It is not with pleasure I recount that one of the few remaining charms of this place is in the form of a red, public phone booth, and this, too, is not without its inevitable degeneration in its solicitations of dubious calling services. I am writing you this note instead.

And then there is the new Tate Modern, the newest prostitute getting hip to the streets....

Professionally speaking however, I am impressed by the ubiquity of the brand in the Londoner's consciousness, its trace found on every street corner market/newsstand, its stamp of endorsement on the gateway of every outing. And so it is I shall leave this place. But I wonder, beyond all the transparencies, has life changed much in being here, or elsewhere?

Then of course there are the comings and goings of my meaningless scribblings. I flip through its pages like a man defeated.

You should not worry. All this is really the epistolary side of me. What more? I shall start work again and I will no longer have these thoughts.

Take care of yourself.

London

Athens,

The promptness of your reply is admirable. I have been unable to do likewise, no doubt as a result of my constant circumnavigation. And like many ancient Greek philosophers, I apologize.

I am not sure that I have fully shed the vestiges of the former life. The new life, if I may call it that, is still something of a wonderment, for better, for worse.

The literary reference was nice, thank you. Yes, it seems this city may have its way with me after all, and again. Useless to fight it, though I am not making myself particularly vulnerable. As far as my innocence is concerned, if indeed there still remained any in me, has all but left. There may be something to tell in all of this, as the expression goes (only as far as the expression goes), having already kissed.

On your end, I hope you will find the time and space to unwind and refuel before the beginning of another academic year.

By the way, though I don't know your father, perhaps he did right in purchasing his little piece of land, despite your criticism of to what it amounts. We are all trying to find our little places, even if it is a little dilapidated.

Take good care.

Casablanca

Amsterdam,

I received your letter. It seems you have been pondering many questions. I appreciate your frankness. I wonder, however, if I am capable of responding. My thoughts on the subject are varied, especially as it concerns such delicate matters. First, I think it is good that you have recorded these things. Despite myself, I still feel it is the best way of confronting one's thoughts. And language comes only with use, as sure as I can attest from my present foreign dwelling.

It is as if at the crossroads we had made a turn, but as the roads converge in the end, we find ourselves at a place we thought we had passed. This leaves us with the feeling that decisions are not final, even useless to take on. Absurd when we think of the pains we had gone through in order to arrive there.

Sometimes we weigh the good and bad. Other times, we just go with our intuition. Who knows when we are right, when we are wrong? But after many of the same lessons, we start to lose a certain sense. Towards the end of your reflection in your letter, you are employing a strange sort of equation. Sometimes we simply need to say, this is my house; it is cheap and unsound, but I will not let animals destroy it.

I have learned, nothing is unforgivable except insincerity. With honesty, even the wasted years can be atoned. Otherwise, one might be in trouble.

In your case, if I may permit myself, the promise of success or happiness seems poisoned by the general climate in which you surround yourself. I think of the others who have entered that network. They share a common denominator in their work, their aspirations, their thirst for the industry, if not dependency, as it sounds like in your case.

As for the girl, there is no need for you to see her, or anyone. And it is only when you have realized that there is no such need, will you start receiving these people for who they are, and not who you project them to be. In my view, one cannot be defined by such a relationship. That is to say, a relationship will not deign to assume that responsibility. We must make ourselves worthy. This recalls the despairing man praying to the godhead to be saved. In the end, only when he is prepared to be saved will he deserve it. And on that day, he might discover that his salvation had already come.

Having said all that, I am sure you will figure it out. And so it goes, my thoughts respond to those of yours without much direction. In any case, I hope you had a nice journey into the country and that you have returned refreshed and strong.

Toulouse

London,

>Once again I have taken up the pen.
>Poetry, and madness. But which came first?

Forgive me my vanity in quoting myself. These words came to mind. Or, perhaps I would do better in saying, As a dog returneth to his vomit, I, too, return....

Paris

Berlin,

Thank you for your letter. It was waiting for me when I arrived from my two weeks in North Africa. Casa, by the way, was a bit rough, if not interesting. I realized I could lose myself in such a place, like many places of like magnificence.

I recall having something of a moment when I became aware of the peculiarity: I was an American, born in Korea, living in France, traveling through Morocco, attending an exhibit on German Bauhaus at a Kasbah in Fez.

Then there was the smiling boy selling cigarettes along the café terraces....

All this, but still, contrary to what you believe, I do not know how much it has to do with my being brave. It is nice of you to think so, regardless. I write this as I make passage through a coastal resort in southern France, off-season and empty. A tiny and hidden restaurant, La Bohème, provides a table.

I shall call on you again as I round up my voyage. I should hope I would have more news.

Saint Tropez

New York,

Enclosed herewith are the slides you have requested. They are of the paintings I had done during that period of reclusion when I lived in the warehouse district. I realize this is a part of my life of which I had spoken very little. It seemed a much more private affair, this thing.

The first set of panels are entitled, *Cinq Cognacs*. The second set of five, *Night and the Circumstance*. The last set, *l'Homme Est Né Libre*, was originally in five panels like the others, of which only two now remain in existence. You may recall, the left panel was published under a pseudonym as a cover image for *Arcade*.

I apologize for initially questioning your intention when you had asked for these slides. I simply did not understand your interest in them. I send them to you now. And with this gesture, perhaps we can put aside that conversation once and for all.

The painting, as well as that general period of my life, I have considered to be a closed chapter. At least for the time. I had told myself I needed to resolve certain things prior to taking all that on again.

In the meantime, I trust I won't encounter these pieces in some renegade expo in Soho, as they seem of little interest to the public.

There it is. I hope you find them to your liking.

Aix-en-Provence

Managua,

I am profoundly sorry to hear you are going through some uncertain times. I wonder if these things could not be the precursors for change. One might hope. In the end, your honesty is commendable, courageous. And my response, undoubtedly inadequate.

I want to say I understand. There are things in this world that bring tears to our eyes. And I realize again in saying this that my life, in essence, is one that is melancholic and solitary. I wonder if there is some universality to this.

I seem to recall floating through human spheres without always being fully present. Here, being in France, it relates more to a cultural interest rather than an interest strictly social. A part of me feels that I have already experienced a little of everything in some sort of strange microcosm of an accelerated time frame. Somewhere, I have left my mark. And I, in turn, have been equally marked. Perhaps these are the things which make up our lives, these little exchanges.

In the end, I believe it is about making peace with ourselves and with those around us, before passing on.

Without sounding too simplistic, I want to convey that I have no doubt your medical complications will resolve themselves. I believe this.

You will also overcome the other struggles in your own fashion. I have faith in you.

One of these days, we will get it right. Until next time, please, please take very good care.

Paris

Minneapolis,

I was happy to finally make your acquaintance after several occasions where we had crossed paths in different settings.

Attentive with your words and gestures of nothing at all, you made me feel completely present. I should tell you how rare this is for me. Our exchange was endearing.

I recall I almost stumbled when you took me under the large brim of your hat to kiss me good night. It was as if I had entered your private dwelling. It was more intimate than I expected and I was veritably transported, a long awaited reprieve from my world.

And your exquisite smile at the thing to which you had rendered me, cast me even further into that oblivion.

What can I say? If it comes to pass that we meet again, I shall be quite happy.

Saint Paul

Seattle,

I know my recent e-mails have been terribly inadequate. I have been typing them on the fly, often on foreign keyboards. This one may be no different. I apologize in advance.

I did meet up with our friend last weekend. It was very good to see her. We went out for some drinks, then more drinks. Europe has turned me into something of a lush, it seems.
It was good to see someone from the old world to reassured me somehow that I had indeed moved on. Someone has witnessed my new surroundings. New life of sorts.

By the way, stop your crying. I do hope things are better. And soon. For you, I mean. For me too.

We will speak again.

Geneva

Los Angeles,

Thank you for your recent letter. I want to say I understand if that does not reduce the situation. Even here, the late night speak-easy couch sits conspicuous in the corner with its third upholstered leg. We have been given the finger repeatedly. It's time to retreat to the cabin in the country.

Sorry to hear about the IRS catching up with you. We will need to get more creative tax accountants for the next fiscal year. Los Angeles can have its inevitable downward spiral, even in the most auspicious of conditions. This is why the only remaining condolence for the industry people is in the form of a big, black Mercedes. Also, I can imagine what you mean about the producer and his ideas. The briefing of the forthcoming production was enough to derange my sensibility.

You must remember: Absurdity was in the '90s. Today, it's Irony.

As far as your idea for the book, I will be the last to endorse such an endeavor, speaking purely from my own misery. The subject you are pondering is particularly disconcerting. Films like that are a reconstitution of the meaningless, and I am not speaking in some existential modality. To write a book about its sin would be to reconstitute the reconstitution of that very absence of meaning – resulting in a kind of processed meaty canned product with undisclosed ingredients found at a late night grocer. That would be the ultimate, not only of the absurd, but also the ironical. I do understand your disdain, and I agree – I myself having picked up the poem again.

My advice is to watch Fellini's *8 1/2* again. This will flush all the vomit down the toilet. Then a little *Amarcord* as disinfectant. Finally, the point is not to despair too much. Your stipend is still more than what most of us are making. And, before you can surmount the afflictions of your being bound to the Fat Man, first get a handle on your free time. Only then with your gathered force can you combat these people. Just humor them a bit for the time. Eventually, the break will be inevitable, if not on your doing, on theirs.

Please take care of yourself. Talk to you soon.

Cannes

San Francisco,

Hello. I don't know if I had fully congratulated you on the new direction which you have secured for yourself. I admire what you are doing, if you will allow me to be vicariously gratified (seeing as I have not been very productive with my own work).

I enclose the latest edition of the manuscript. As it stands, still a ways to go. Given its state of incompleteness, you will think it vain on my part to have bound it. I suppose something in me needed to see it in this form. And, though I would be the last to solicit any feedback, whatever response from your end would be greatly appreciated. I feel I have been alone with this thing for so long I no longer know what it is, what it has become.

As for the rural east, there is not much to recount. Though in the recesses of my consciousness, something tells me that there was a poet here. I sense his presence near me.

I hope your work is treating you well. Perhaps we can uphold some sort of correspondence, even if only sporadically.

Best wishes for the holidays. I am sure the coast is charming this time of year.

New Haven

New York,

It is always nice to receive your letters. I am pleased to hear your studies are going well. I hope your job situation can also evolve into something better, though I wonder about such agents.

And me? Many things, many things, it seems.

First, I would have you know, that sort of intrigue is not spoken here – not in a language I can decipher anyway. The *cabbages* are not yet ripe. I am encountering some interesting times, nonetheless.

I am coming up on a year here, but still, there is a certain surreal element in all of this. Sometimes I wonder if there is not a part of me wanting to see a familiar face. Despite all this, I am beginning to meet people at a comfortable rate – a rate which seems to appeal both to my sense of reticence and my sense of not wanting to lose complete contact with the world.

All this, and still, behind the face of a city that boasts 350 days of sunshine out of 365 days a year, there drifts a manic-depressive cloud threatening passive-aggressive. These are all very clinical terms, I know.

So I grace through this life tentatively, though not entirely insecure. It is along these poles I have tied my hammock, pastis in hand.

I know that our interactions have been minimal in the past. Still, you have done more than most even with your few salutations. This is my way of saying I have appreciated your persistence. I have recently come to realize friendships cannot withstand testing. I have not known many, just a few, but such ones extraordinary. I am presently resuming one here.

I leave you with such perplexing words. You were expecting nothing less. I do hope you are well and sound. I trust you have not forgotten how to enjoy yourself as you approach your quarter century. Happy Birthday.

I look forward to hearing from you again.

Marseille

Seoul,

I wish I could relate what is happening. Nothing new on the one hand, and yet, I am seeing everything again as if for the first time. I feel confounded. I am fated to finish the rest of my days in this place; Or, I am leaving on the next plane. I have written my last word; I have yet another life of writing ahead of me. There is nothing to be gained here, like elsewhere. I am punishing myself. Between desire and the object, there is a vast divide. But enough, I am indulging.

I have applied for a position in Paris with some misgivings. Chance will lead me to my next place, for I no longer seem to know for myself, or care. In spite of everything, I still have the minimum to survive, albeit with difficulty.

And, as it turns out, my writing – or not writing – has become an insignificant detail of this overwhelming senselessness.

On another order of business, the perennial rapport with my spiritual brother still seems to hold. I have recently been declared the godfather of his expected child. We are, however, repeating some of the old conversations from our early years: *What are we doing here?* He says he wants to be a shepherd in Scotland. This seems more admirable than my petty vision of being a poet in Paris. Between him and myself, there is a great divide, as seems between all brothers. He still prefers I stay here without much prospect. He painted such a terrible picture of an asshole working for a living that I no longer know any more.

And how are you in the midst of all this? Marriage? Can you read my handwriting? Life of Art/non Art. The only sublime thing untainted by my terrible disposition – the weather, the glorious weather. Unbelievable, this, my life.

I hope you are better than I am.

Aix-en-Provence

New York,

Your letter, having first made the journey via one of my past dwellings and twice the greater half of three oceans, arrived belated, but not unwelcomed.

True, I did not expect to hear from you, our conversations in the past having always been perfunctory. I am aware that my relationship (and perhaps too, your own) with your sister rendered things uneasy, regrettably impeding our proper association independent of hers. I do appreciate you extending yourself. I always understood you to be more thoughtful than myself.

I shall not attempt to make excuses for the unfolding of that exchange in which she and I took part. It had become tiresome. Many unpardonable incidences in my life have resurfaced as of late. This is one which remains among the more sour in flavor.

I should have known. I still see your eyes, widening in disbelief as your sister conducted the evening when the three of us first made our acquaintance. She exhibited a great force. I was too stupidly impatient to recognize in you the force much more subtle and dignified – true.

And now, rendered sufficiently ill at ease knowing that you are privy to these accounts, I shall not try to hide what has long since been exposed. The greater part of this regret is that ultimately the affinities were perhaps more closely aligned between you and me – the truth of which we are not to discover. I shall not presume that this correspondence will contradict my notion, but I do hope in any case that we may continue.

Sincerely,

London

The Hague,

Nice to hear back from you. I am glad the letter was forwarded. I trust your tour of America was in good turn. Now you are settling in Europe, for the time. A job, etc. You are putting your degree to good use.

As for myself, after some traveling of my own, I have immersed myself in Paris. It is here I shall find the center of my solitude (as if the solitude I had known in the past was not of the central kind). What else shall I find? This I leave to the locals to decide.

And yes, I would love to see you out here, even if you intend on bringing your lover. I want to meet this person. He must be extraordinary to deserve your affection.

Be well. I hope to speak to you again soon.

Paris

Copenhagen,

I had a vague notion your birthday was near. If this is true, then Happy Birthday. If I am mistaken, it still seemed a good pretext for this letter.

It has been a little over three months that I have been here. Apart from some traveling, I have situated myself for the time. But still, I am unsettled, as I continue to question what it is I am doing. But where else could I be? Indeed, we are like the mustard seeds....

It is true, I am not really writing. Did I ever think I could have finished the poem? Maybe I am simply pulling myself together after my social suicide. Maybe I am playing the role of the fugitive after having murdered Art. Even my childhood dream of painting is eluding me once again. I have held it for nearly two decades and all that there remains is its vestige, worn. But then again, I suppose none of this really matters.

How are you? And your studies?

I do hope you are staying warm and safe. I should say that despite everything, this side of Europe has been as welcoming as I could have hoped. Perhaps it is just me, stubborn and desperate. If you make it down here, I have no doubt they would find you infinitely more charming.

Take good care of yourself. I will speak to you again soon.

Dijon

Evanston,

I received your message, thank you. You are finding yourself in the rural mid-west. I hope you are able to get some rest which you deserve.

Of late, and possibly for the first time in many years, I have been feeling intimidated by others and my surroundings. I ruminate conversations in my head, running through imaginary dialogues. I am like a boy again, trembling at the presence of the unfamiliar.

Then there is all the brouhaha of holidays approaching.

All in all, it is much like I imagined here. Still I am finding little recognition in hindsight, as if some respite were required to look back properly.

The english colloquy is slipping from my constitution, surely at the same rate I am acclimating to the new tongue. And Faust, dear Faust, like a stale odor from the past.... Art happens. My life is playing itself out like that old paradox, at once familiar and strange. One begins to wonder about reconciliation.

Happy New Year. I will be in touch.

Barcelona

Carro,

Belated my reply, yes. One of these days you will understand all this. I certainly haven't figured it out for myself. Many reasons for which I am unable to respond in general – none of which are very substantial.

After a few weeks of being busy with work, I am picking up all the scrap verses I had left dormant. As far as your letter – "happy as a bird" (sic.) – and a bit sad, too? I find recognition in your words. It reminded me of this postcard of Chagall. I enclosed it herewith.

My time here has been alternating from difficult to very difficult. Work-wise, I am beginning to make my contacts. I have been doing some consulting. I put together some environmental campaigns for an organization and a photo book project concerning polio. But somehow, all of these things do not seem to add up. I am still thinking of Italy. France. Morocco....

I finally received news of the family: I am now thrice an uncle and a godfather. Can't say I am deserving, or even feeling up to it. We will see as these little ones start growing.

I hope things are good with your newly found freedom. How else have you been passing your time? Work is still treating you well?

I wish for you to find your place. Cities can be cruel – people too. Somehow the world crowds around us and this, I am convinced, more than anything, is what makes us lonely. As for me, I feel another period of reclusion coming on. This, too often, is my response to the affliction. With your permission, I take solace in knowing you exist.

Nomads, indeed, all of us. And your closing salutation was quite nice, thank you. I appreciate your thoughts.

You will help keep me inspired, and in touch.

Soon.

New York

Rome,

Thank you for your e-mail, and the dirt on your housemate. I was precisely feeling a little out of the loop. I had been wondering about the variety of suitors who were bound to loiter about the parlor.

As for me, however, I am sorry to say I cannot reciprocate by way of relating any romance that may have unfolded from this side of the Mediterranean. None have unfolded. – Nay, if you insist, there was a brief (and innocent) encounter with a friend of a friend of a friend. She and I were caught in a tight passage in an underground club, a veritable bottleneck towards the bar. We were pressed up against each other but she didn't seem to mind so terribly. She asked me with her enormous eyes, "Why did you come to France?" – No reason, no reason at all. She had lips like mine and I wondered what it would be like to kiss her. But, alas, she asked me to dance, and I declined.... That's it for now. Sorry, that wasn't much of a story.

The weather has been quite nice here. It is difficult to gauge the passing of seasons. I find it hard to believe it is already mid-December. And, despite all the mantra and the ubiquitousness of holiday preludes, I sometimes forget that the grand changing of guards for the millennium is at hand. And with this disjointed *cahot* in space and time and climate comes a sense of displacement.

And so it is in those slight moments of transformation, quietly in a café as I observe the encroachment of evening outside when the din of this other language subdues the room.... No, I must stop pretending that I am a writer. I apologize for the awkwardness of this letter. Perhaps it is due to my state of pensiveness, and the gradual recession of the English tongue from my immediate sphere. Truly I am a foreigner, here and elsewhere.

I have become a stranger in this city. Incognito. Incommunicado. – Save but the proprietary relationship with my host, brother, minister of culture, and now, business partner.

Happy Holidays. Be good, and take care of yourself.

Ciao, ciao.

Paris

New York,

I am well, thank you. It was truly nice to hear from you, though I am sorry about the terrible side of your recent existence. That city does not cease to malign the innocent. It is cosmopolitan that way. You must speak out.

I've dropped a small fortune on my relocation in order to recreate the comforts once found in my most auspicious times. I will soon be taken to task, to smell the glove, as it were, of my folly. Already a drunken evening has passed against which I have sworn never to repeat. It is as such here, at once intoxicating and sobering, the old and the new, the tiny and the grand, the beautiful and the heinous, *la belle noiseuse,* the good-bad-and-ugly all come together in harmony like a fantastic western. Leone was right.

It snowed here this weekend – an aberration unseen in over a decade, sending the local authorities scrambling for subsidies. People are saying that I brought it with me. *El niño,* I pleaded. They didn't understand.

And so it goes, the loneliness of travel....

I shall regard you with some affection as we all strive to find our little places in the world. We shall slowly overcome. The pilgrimage begins and ends.

Well, darling, I shall write again. Until next time,

Aix-en-Provence

Boston,

It is true we are not on the same page. But this much had been understood. I apologize for not responding adequately to your letter, or in the way you would have had me respond. It may be that I shall never know of your expectations.

A long time ago, I wanted you to understand that part of me which was, and still remains, the greater half of my constitution. When I had realized that I could not expect this, the other things didn't really seem to matter: My writing you letters at first, and then stopping; my not giving you flowers; you asking for the prints; you writing me that long letter, then me not responding properly – what does all this mean? I don't know. You might imagine the various letters and responses in which I would have marveled during the other part of our relationship. But that seems extraneous at this point.

I know this much: You had spoken your peace with your last words; you had spoken your peace for us both.

Perhaps this is farewell. I had not imagined it this way. But then again, so little seems to turn out as we imagine.

Minneapolis

Zurich,

Sorry about your recent mishap. I can tell you I know of what you speak. I have my own deadline coming up at breakneck speed, after which I will freeze and die, then come back to some semblance of living to finish the project. The stress is getting to be a little too much, I have to say. Your production manager can tell you what happens when they have to reschedule a printing date. It costs less to cut off someone's head than to stop a Heidelberg press.

Other than that, I am well. Despite all the booze.

And how are you?

New York

Moscow,

Thank you for your lovely story. It was almost like I was there. As far as rides on the handlebars, I know some steep hills we could go on. I only wonder if we know each other well enough.

Ah, the days have been accelerated. Down to just weeks before I leave this big mess, passport in hand. What will become of us all? I apologize for this moment of glee. I have so much I would like to tell you. Place and time....

Meanwhile, I look forward to speaking to you again soon. I still have a little time here before my departure. What else would I do?

> *Il n'y a plus de roues de bicyclette.*
> There are no more bicycle wheels.
> — Beckett

Minneapolis

Paris,

In your bold inquiry into the makings of the poem (and also its author) you pose some arresting questions. Normally, I don't make a practice of responding to letters from unknown sources, especially as it concerns matters rather personal. But so poignant is your gaze into everything inexplicable, I now challenge myself to reply.

If only I could speak more fluently about my writing, and the perceived shortcomings of my romantic (or unromantic) life. If only we lived in a perfect world....

It is true, there exists an undeniable rapport between my work, my life, and the relationships that have resounded through the various turns of these parallel paths.

In your words you demonstrate an awareness that is rare. I sense also a kind of existential melancholy at play on your end. The vocabulary you employ in your exposition, your discourse on compassion in an apparently meaningless world...the ensemble comes together to arouse a sentiment in me long since latent. In any case, you compose a compelling piece. I appreciate the frankness with which you speak. I oblige myself to do the same, despite my reservation in communicating via this medium epistolary which can inspire the imagination to aspire beyond that which can claim footing in reality.

True beauty is never conventional. And love does not involve appearances. I am convinced you possess it, this beauty, even with the little that I know, the little that you disclose. You need not expend your introspection around this.

I have always had difficulty speaking of myself. This requires distance, and perspective. If I can relate to you some things, I suppose I, too, have spent the greater part of my life alone. (This was the first point of identification with your letter). Granted, my being alone was a choice, a measure of gravity with which I decided to lead my life. I had funded my days with books, art, travel, work...coffee and cigarettes – anything to lessen the feeling of solitude which was ubiquitous, even in the presence of others. Now, I question the cause and effect of my disposition and my life situation. I have had my share of relations which did not last, often of my own doing, or undoing. For whatever reason, I had never felt transformed in the way that I had imagined true intimacy would be. I am obviously remarking a certain lack, which was to be the essential premise of such separations. Without any pretense of being selfless, I often found myself in situations where I felt compelled to disengage myself from others, on their behalf – I, often having been the first to acknowledge my shortcomings.

The few intimate exchanges which I had encountered had taken place during the period of my life when I was anything but sedentary. Constantly moving, I was towing an epic poem I was to never really finish, only abandon – this thing having evolved into something more of an excuse than an endeavor. My last three years were spent in Europe tethered to much of the same routine, only in a different climate, (unfortunate we did not cross paths then) before returning here to New York this past summer. I am still trying to figure out if this is where I need to be. I suppose

I am waiting for a sign of sorts. Even as I believe in self-affirmation, and the notion of making a significant act, I also believe there are things beyond our immediate control. What I mean is that I would like to create something of a home for myself, if indeed this place will have me.

I try to convince myself I need to be in this city to get this work published. My residence here, however, has been fruitless for the time. The poem, though I have been known to play it down, or even deny it all together, remains the single most important thing. Clearly this makes further reference to my unfurnished history in the realm of romance. One cannot live long with two lovers before having one become jealous of the other. So it seems.

I realize I am saying a lot, and at the same time, nothing at all. You speaking of love and being loved may have been the second and more important point of identification. How could I resist?

Love is undoubtedly the greatest achievement in life. What else can there be? To find contentment, even joy, companionship... all these things are worthwhile, but without some higher calling, seem meaningless. I am aware of the lack of authority with which I speak – this thing before which I am completely mystified and at the same time utterly disillusioned. And ultimately it goes against my nature to persist. But still, like a true skeptic, I linger, incredulous, testing its properties. I used to believe I would one day find that true love. And on that day, I would cease to communicate, having at last arrived at understanding. Today, I no longer know, or claim to know. It is that scholarship, and the profession of knowing nothing, and the slow (cold) hemlock charting its finite path. You, soon to be professor, might understand. This is perhaps the language of the "pale criminal": *The chalk streak stopped the hen. The streak that he himself struck, stopped his poor reason.* "Madness after the deed" was how he referred to it.

I am subsequently reminded of Rilke who had ultimately experienced the affection of the woman whom Nietzsche tried to woo. She was perhaps wise in her choosing. May we all be so wise. And as concerns the scenario at hand, it suffices to say my fortune resembles more closely that of the philosopher than the poet. My misfortune. Insufferable thing.

As for you, I cannot help but sense the tragedy in your own past which you have survived. You are stronger now. Brave for making your way, as well. I trust you are finding things better, finding what you need – at least in part. We are travelers. And in our travels we seek our semblables, those with whom we can share a part of our lives. One could only wish.

I will leave you with this. I shall be terribly curious as to know your opinion on all this matter. I wonder whether you will in turn find enough affinity to reply.

In any case, please be well. I hope to speak to you more.

New York

Venice,

I have visited your writings again. I hope that's all right. Tempestuous they are.

I was quite glad hearing of your happiness (though coming and going). And in your sadness, how I want to reach out.

I will look you up soon, possibly incite a remote kiss, if I may.

Until then, wishing you are well.

More to follow.

Seoul

Las Vegas,

By now you must be getting settled. I do not know this city, but I have come to learn in my various moves, the space we create inside of ourselves can overcome our surroundings. This is why I told you that you are beautiful. I suspect my inspiration came from a variety of sources. Our last exchange was endearing, and I was left with a light sort of feeling.

My mother has arrived, and I have been good to accommodate her schedule in my small apartment. She will be with me for another month. They say that there is a special relationship between mother and son. This we shall see.

I hope your transition goes smoothly. Your uncle will recognize just how precious you are – something your parents were not capable of doing. Then you can call that place home. With your consent, we will continue this and it will be like I am there with you.

Until next time, you will take good care of yourself. I will speak to you soon.

Boston

Mexico City,

It seems I owe you a letter. You will understand that I am not so fluent in these things. Something in me is uneasy, even without the aid of my circumstances.

I cannot give you a detailed account of my days if only out of shame that my days are composed of little, if nothing at all. I can say that I have had much time to reflect, but also that such reflection has led me back to myself. I turn and turn and everything remains quite the same. I feel like Rimbaud, but less impassioned. Like Hart Crane, but weaker. Like Stevens, but with less knowing. I have come short in many ways. I feel like Kafka, but more frightened – at last, I have outdone someone. Were I some sort of transcendentalist, things would be simpler. That is to say I have found a sort of loneliness, a sister to the solitude I had known before, and I can only hope that she would recognize this pathos and look upon me with some kindness.

I will try to convey more in my next correspondence.

I hope all is well.

Paris

Madrid,

I was worried to hear of your predicament. It is possible some of us have been born outside of what is commonly known as society. I feel this way too often to think otherwise. It is a mark. It is recognized among like people. And I recognize it in you. This is why I have always imagined knowing you even after becoming too old to remember anything.

I realize I was overly suggestive in the past without fully understanding the situation. What I really meant to say is that it is perfectly fine to feel the way you are feeling. And that whatever you decide will be all right, that your actions need not be justified in other people's eyes. This one prerogative remains yours.
You are not your fault. I will canonize this expression.

Write me as often as you like. I will do my best to respond.

New York

Naples,

Subject at rest...remains at rest.

It seems I have fallen into my old ways. Things are troubling. I still think of France, and my writing. I have not been disciplined enough to consider the books I have pulled from my shelves.

Have you received the manuscript?

There is less and less here for me, I realize this now. This time, unlike other times – so I believe – is beyond the mere physicality of my existence. Perhaps it has always been so, and I am simply getting older. I have been going out less than ever. Even when I was living in Boston, knowing no one, it seemed I felt more connected with things around me. An extreme lethargy and an overall malaise have descended upon me that I do not know my next move.

Life without charm.

I have been thinking of your invitation to see the millennium passage from the Sahara. We may not survive until the new year the way fate will have us. The desert sky may be the only thing left of this world when we are gone.

Minneapolis

Portland,

I am sorry. The last time we spoke, it made me a little sad to hear things were not as well as they could have been, as well as you deserve. I hope things are better.

I just started production again. It will be the last. This I have promised myself.

I have not had much time to write. Not much time to do anything. I am doing the work of two people on my own.
I am doing the work of two months in one. All this will pass.

All this will pass. You should tell yourself this, too. I would let you, if you like.

Paris

Minneapolis,

Your letter (hand delivered by your messenger friend) came to me as bitter sweet. Forgive me for the belated reply. (You did not include your new address.) I hope this letter is forwarded to your place.

I myself am looking to move for December. I have located a small apartment by the Cathedral. A part of me wanted to get out of the downtown area. I am not sure what this change will do for me but, as it happens, I had already given my landlord notice to vacate this present dwelling. The thing about a mid-life crisis is that it comes early, takes on many forms, and does not deign to go away. Perhaps I will ground myself someday, somewhere.

I hope your studies are going well. You have made great progress. Still, I should admit that I worry about you from time to time. I know you will take good care of yourself.

I hope to see you soon.

Saint Paul

Avignon,

Last night I walked in the rain – sweet, sweet rain. I thought of us, slightly afraid of this terrifying happiness.

I dreamt I reclined in your passenger seat and you seduced me with a flung scarf.

I whispered in your ear: Press Conference. You made me smile and I was with hope.

I want to ride your carousel. I want to win stuffed animals for you.

London

Lyon,

Nice to run into you during your passage through Paris (though I imagine there have been more auspicious encounters). Were it not for your natural graces, the atrocities committed in your liquored state would deserve a thrashing. You fell on me repeatedly, not to mention the lame attempts to separate me from my drink. All that, and still I was charmed.

Jesting aside. To answer your question, I reside now in the Latin Quarter near the Sorbonne. I remain faithfully in the Left Bank with only occasional afternoons in Beaubourg. I have stopped frequenting Le Fumoir, having been specifically requested by an ex-girlfriend. The women are very territorial that way. They call the shots here and I am left with no choice other than to respect her wishes, however capricious.

Thank you for the word of the exhibition. I will make the effort of being there.

Paris

Charlottesville,

Precocious, yes. And with such daring.

I hesitated prior to responding knowing this much: It is one thing when a younger woman seeks to make the acquaintance of an older man; it seems an entirely different matter when that same older man pursues the companionship of that younger woman. (Forgive me if I seem to be invoking a convention.) In the society in which we live, the male-female relational disparity is even more exaggerated when in the case of being amended by the latter clause.

I was your age fourteen years ago. Perhaps equally precocious – equally eager in my precociousness. As a result, I felt outside, not only of my age group, but of everyone around me. That period of my life has marked me more than any other. Perhaps I identify with you to this extent.

I was impressed with your perceptiveness, even prior to having acknowledged your age. Your words stood out as intelligent, real. Honest. This is rare in life, and certainly through this particular vehicle of interaction where everything remains hidden and anonymity is king. You neglected to describe yourself as brave. Still, precociousness is not the word I would use to roundabout your act of making contact.

If I know anything about the culture at large, I suspect you are in your current life being overwhelmed by solicitations by suitors who seek the affection of a younger, attractive and intelligent lady. Here, I must distinguish myself from these others. In my heart of hearts, it is probable that I desire to meet you – a desire undoubtedly more fervent than I am prepared to project. My present response to your letter, however, is in an effort to forestall any potential error on my part. Surely I will succeed in convincing you before convincing myself.

Enough then – I shall leave you with these words. Thank you. Please be well, and take care.

Cambridge

Jerusalem,

It has been a few months since our correspondence, outside of a few straggling e-mails. Yes, I have indeed restored that old motorcycle. Meanwhile, it is getting cooler in the evenings and the riding season will come to an end. Still, I felt I needed to widen my circles, at least in my geography.

I am in the grips of another production deadline. Late nights, long hours. Still writing. Still trying to write.

You are well? I understand that you have met someone.
I am not sure I was supposed to know this, but I was happy to hear it. These words are not without some sense of unease.
(I do not think I am being presumptuous.) Perhaps we shall learn through other people. In any case, I would value the persistence of our friendship.

I am proud of you for having fearlessly gone out there and having achieved the things you have, the job, the art, the community of friends.

Keep me posted. Until next time,

Philadelphia

Saint Paul,

I thought of you today. I thought of you yesterday, as well.

I think you have infected me. A benign sort of infection.
It makes my heart feel light.

This is extraordinary. Already I am writing you letters.
And just days before our lips meet again. Mine are wetted with
anticipation. All of this comes to me very dearly. And I can
only hope to know you more deeply, intensely – in all the ways
you would have me know you. The fallen angel and I have
this much in common: There is no separating the body and
the soul. Ours will meet in the eventual fire. Chemistry, yes.
And a little alchemy, too.

In reading the lines on my hand, you had prophesied a certain
measure of love. Though I have never been known to heed such
fortunes told, I believe you because you have said so. The power
seems equally in your hands, so to speak.

Regardless of how my future will unfold, I liked it simply because
you held my hand.

Minneapolis

Perth,

It was good to hear your voice, despite the delay and traffic of passing motor bikes, delivery trucks. It is odd writing you, not knowing when you will receive this letter. I admit, I have not been good about writing, letters or otherwise.

I have worried about you. I suspect the evenings have their weight in the stars, in the absence of stars. Perhaps you long for home, or think you are without. I believe you will endure these things and come out for the better. As for myself, I cannot yet say what will become of me.

Someone once said that when one travels, one does not leave a place and the people behind, but that they leave a part of themselves. Maybe that is why I fear traveling, as if I had nothing left to leave behind. I say this as I sit in a hotel lobby, uncertain of my next move / non-move.

Anyway, I simply wanted to acknowledge our last exchange. I seal this note and drop it in the mail, lest I sit on it for too long and decide everything has changed. I should hope that I would know more of my situation soon.

Rabat

Paris,

I realize I am much more delicate than I would have liked to consider. Your last visit continues to anguish me.

There was that moment in our interaction when I felt a distinct shift in you behavior, in your regard. A look of such intoxication, as if a lifetime of sadness had converged upon you all at once and you gazed at me with eyes imploring.

I had accompanied you to your hotel where you had insisted on not being alone that night. If we did not fall into a repetition of our old ways, it was not because chivalry was at my side. I know myself well enough to say I would have been defenseless to any advances on your part. You alone were the heroine of this episode.

I recall in the morning you conducted yourself with exceptional grace, and with the appropriate measure of acknowledgement of the uneasy moment which had passed between us, for which you seemed to feel responsible.

Please, it is here that I acknowledge the great uneasiness which was of my doing, alone.

I am sorry.

New York

Prague,

Thank you so much for the extraordinary book. An excellent find, one that only you could have made. I had read it immediately and was so delighted. It was exactly what I needed.

Otherwise, I am still out of work. I hope to be hearing back from one company where I recently interviewed – a position referred to me by a friend.

I should hope that I would be ready to apply myself in the field again.

I am glad I was able to host you during your visit. (Though what I did could hardly be considered hosting.)

Thank you again for the marvelous gift.

London

Algiers,

Indeed my letters are few, far between – fewer by the two not reaching you, including the one where I relate to you my new address. I pass it on again.

Your writing has come a long way. Its substance betrays many nights peering into the darkened sepulcher, and its words, a familiarity with the demons. I myself feel inadequate to comment on them. Your new friends are Kierkegaard, Rilke, and the many eastern European fatalists.

Concerning myself, I have been reading. I have started *Citadelle*, and am finding it good. And though I feel it building something in me, I fear in my present state of preoccupation, it may be difficult to make much progress.

It turns out I am bound to stay through April because my mother will be making her way here, not unlike her extended visit several years ago. It seems her intuition received signals of her son's descent. Her false pretext of business in the city cannot hide her motive to save me from a desperate situation as her itinerary conveniently includes an extended layover.

Given this, I do not think I will ever get out of this city. Perhaps I shall petition for amnesty. It may take nothing less than a U.N. resolution for my departure.

On your end, it looks like you will also be greeted by a visitor shortly. I understand she has had her share of ups and downs recently. And as such, you two will get along dangerously well – though in part, I fear, at my expense.

I do appreciate your letters. I hope that my low frequency of response is not taken the wrong way. I find so little solace in anything, and my energy is quite depleted. I have played out the worst scenario in my mind and it will end with my mother not recognizing me upon her arrival.

Paris

New York,

There are certain truths I have discovered: The life of a star is ephemeral.

Anxiety is a post-modern synapse.

Exist, you and I both. Together.

We are not of this universe, but we are from the same universe.

I want to crawl into your wormhole. I want to taste your Poignant Melodic Surprise.

Boston

Cambridge,

Your tireless search for edification is admirable.

But to be learned does not replenish the lack of wit. Education does not belie a lack of understanding. One cannot become enlightened, for there is only becoming. Or, in this case, not very becoming.

Do not be mistaken: there is nothing logical in the absurd, even in your designated metaphysical realm. Absurdity is only as such for its extension outside of logic. Irony is king. Satire is its illegitimate and insufferable offspring. This is all within the context of Wittenstein, and without. It is a proposition by title only. At most, a tautology; at its very least, a truism.

I will make no concession in philosophy, nor in religion. And I happily mix the two as a matter of course, but only during the hours confined to cocktails. I will, however, declare my defeat in an email exchange where the audience is an undisclosed group of hobbyists and the opponent is a rhetorician.

Incidentally, the word "penultimate" is charming when a woman refers to one of two remaining socks as she is disrobing; to use the word "antepenultimate" is a matter entirely different.

Please do not feel insulted. The intent of these words still reside in the sphere of human compassion – if only at its metaphysical realm.

Vienna

Lake Geneva,

Lovely to hear from you. I like the new series you are putting together. Nice to know you are producing. Perhaps there is redemption after all in the prairie lands. And the melancholy you feel is surely some urban anxiety slowed down to a mid-western gait.

By the way, the New York City take-out is overrated. With any practical frequency, it proves itself to be altogether unpalatable.

I have just accepted an art director position at an agency. I am not sure what this will mean in the scope of things, the studio, etc. But the money situation didn't leave much choice in the matter. I suppose moonlighting is not new in my world. I just didn't think my own work would still be secondary after all this time – the same repetitious lament, all but in minor variations.

The new apartment is quite nice. In a strange way, it reminds me of the other place above the deli. The bathroom is private and it is refinished inside, making it a league above the previous boarding house. Funny waking up now only footsteps away from cafés and boutiques. And the landlord is actually quite congenial. He graces me in the corridors with his stories of former tenants.

I think in the next couple weeks there may be some changes in the work arena. I will keep you posted.

New York

Paris,

I gaze into the blackened sky. It offers no reply. I count the leaves that drift past my feet. And yes, they are indifferent. And the birds that seem to be in the know, they yield not to my calling. Hopelessly I reflect on these things in the lapse between my being and my oblivion.

As I stay up alone in the apartment, I can't help but look around and think how there still remains suspension by way of accommodations un-furnished with mismatched chairs in the backdrop of curtains slowly drooping, projects un-finished, dropped proposals still loitering, prospects un-pursued, a manuscript torn, scrolling past the numbers of contacts at the publishing house, many things which lie powerless to the *un*-ness of things, the un-willing photo album, the canvases hardly brushed upon, and the camera poised to capture me in all my nakedness, and will I ever make it back to Paris?

What have I become? Do I remain a man? A poet, perhaps?

I shall not be defined by this moment, insufferable.

I am listening to your song with melancholy as the world outside goes about its midnight business in police sirens and car alarms, and traffic and idiots on the roof tops setting off bottle rockets with dogs barking....

Morning will come and sweep away all the garbage and I will have forgotten again.

So be it. I still want you. Let us write a book together. Let us create a world, you and me.

Boston

Bangkok,

It was good to hear from you, though your last postcard from Singapore sounded sad. Sad, yes, but happy too. You are finding loneliness in displacement. Travel seems that way, a heightened sense of everything. I think that is what I fear about traveling. The stars, the space between the stars, the silence between words, the pauses between the ticking of the clock....

I am going through a period, feeling very tenuous about everything around me. Even my writing is not giving me any grounding. Financially, slowly becoming insolvent. Emotionally, very absent other than the anxiety in watching a problem get out of control.

After suffering a sort of breakdown, I have applied to several positions including some arguably more ambitious than I can hope to obtain. Others, safer, though a recent interview with one prospective employer showed me that nothing should be taken for granted.

I have decided, or the situation has decided for me, that if I do not secure work by next month, then I will pack my car and drive to New York where I have arranged with a friend to stay until I figure out what it is I need to do.

The one thing about desperate situations is that clarity will emerge, for better or worse. This, sometimes, is the only thing that allows me to go on. The space between stars....

San Francisco

Budapest,

At last, news from the old world! – Though I had to wade through the "philosophies" and fill in where your pen failed to leave ink. Your reckless knowledge has outdone itself again. It seems all too typical of you to write a letter and carry it for an entire season before mailing it.

You can expand on these thoughts. With your permission, I would publish it in the journal and send you copies.

You can let me know. I will be in touch.

Minneapolis

Seoul,

This was the first time I had heard from you directly since your unfortunate arrest and detention. I understand your followers are petitioning for amnesty. I have been obliged to respond.

I am, however, glad to know that you are well, health-wise.

I was surprised to hear you had taken time to read my work. So it is, you have discovered what the prodigal son has been doing for the last decade. Perhaps now I have procured a place outside the area designated as your shadow.

I do not presume to know what you are going through. Once native, you expedited your exile in being faithful to your forebears, divided in the land you would reconcile. Once free, you secured your tether in being benevolent to others, captive to the people you would set free. Your Christ has led you to bondage. *Forgive them for they know not what they do.* I pray your God will not forsake you in the end.

I wonder whether now in your present state of suspension, we might not resume communication – something which was plainly impossible before.

Boston

Melbourne,

Thank you dearly for your letter. I appreciate everything you have said. It is nice to hear you are well, overall.

On my end, having gone through the simple motions of packing and moving proved to be therapeutic, as if I needed this to fulfill some sort of impulse for change. And in exchange I am finding myself in an unfamiliar spiritual place, only made more poignant by the strange air around me.

I understand more and more how afraid I am of uncertainties, of things unknown. My life at times seems so foreign that to venture beyond my immediate frontier would take considerable courage.

Even the simple rites of waking and proceeding with my day, beyond the speechless routine found of coffee and cigarettes, seem impossible tasks. I see now that my previous travels were primarily out of innocent wanderings, and headless relocations. It is for this that I admire what you are doing.

For my part, I concede that the desire to move is as meaningless as the place in which I find myself. Strange, this endless pursuit of a place.

I have been working on the poem. I sat with it recently and read it through from beginning to end, and in doing so I felt myself shaking visibly. I was not certain if I had come far, or I had come nowhere. And the unsettling feeling, as if it were possible to hold one's entire life between the pages of a book.

I hope all of this does not sound too tiresome. I have carried this letter a week now, writing, re-writing this exposition, hoping to distill some lyrical quality I had assumed in the past. There is something profoundly wrong – certainly at present – though I suspect it has always been there and I am beginning to see it once again. I cannot apologize enough for the melancholic state in which this letter joins you – the same mood pervasive in the last days of summer for which you had already reproached me.

The curtains have remained closed, though one might imagine the courtyard worth viewing. The Christmas lights on the bushes, I can see them glowing through the blinds. But, as it were, this place, like so many places, is only for the time, and by spring, I should be in a new location.

I will let you know.

New York

Los Angeles,

I am writing you to formally congratulate you on your engagement, to thank you for the invitation, and to apologize for my failure to attend your gathering. And despite the understanding that my last letter to you was not received well – my best intentions remaining suspect – I am also writing to relate my present situation. My increasing discomfort with our phone conversations was becoming more and more evident to me, perhaps also to you.

I am reminded of your gift to me and my thinking that I wanted to give you something of myself in turn. However, I see I am not ready to deliver this, or to reciprocate your motions in any way.

I am having difficulty in reconciling the things you said before and whatever present initiative you mean to take to whatever end. Although I trust that the end you seek is good, I do not know that I am prepared, or even willing. I had thought that you decided for yourself that I was not the one with whom you would continue to interact.

And although I felt that some of the things you said were unfair, I did not protest, if only to acknowledge that this end was inevitable. Certainly there are enough things about me which would cause you to be upset. I simply didn't understand your timing – or, if I may say so, your interpretation of my last letter, which, at the time, was the best I could do. In spite of the risk of upsetting you further with yet another treaty, I need to remind you of how you were feeling and to say there is no reason you should not continue to harbor those feelings. I am not better now than I was then.

It is not my goal to become another individual who was once a part of your life but is no longer. Still, I cannot disregard the things which have been recently brought into the open. This is my weakness. You will aid me in preventing a recurrence of this past.

I wish you the best.

Boston

London,

I send you the latest edition of Faust. Much of it is similar to the edition you have held. Fifty or so pages cut, another fifty pages rewritten.

Passages in *The Third Quarter*, you may note, are brief meditations loosely based on my preoccupation in Lake Geneva to which you were privy. This part is a late entry for this edition. And though short of doing justice to that evening, certain objectives seemed worth pursuing. Even as I write this, I am more than aware of its shortcomings. I trust your critical eye will discern these things. It is an honor for me to address your interest in my work with the presentation of this manuscript.

I also wanted to thank you again for your generous offer of hospitality, though somehow undermined by my change of plans.

I wish you well for the holidays and the new year as you round out the remaining days of your sabbatical. We might assemble in the near future to continue the discourse.

Paris

New York,

I dreamt of you again.

In the labyrinth of your mysteries, I was lost, and found.

You devised a plan to win my affection.

I was spread against your body's landscape, my cadaver made exquisite by your touch and I was racked between earth and sky, spellbound, compliant.

Your words traversed over centuries to arrive and render me speechless.

You are my beautiful semblable. My more miraculous half.

My desire for you is only second to my love.

Jericho

Chicago,

It was delightful to hear your voice, almost perky with your new found bio-chemical-physiological balance. I hope this letter finds you on the up and up. Though for my part, I continue to suffer my clinical *this* and *that* without treatment, I know you won't hold any of my imbalances against me. My daily medication of coffee, cigarettes, and a book of poems seems to mediate my moods.

Chicago suddenly sounds inviting as you describe it from your new place. I hope to make it over there some time in January, regardless of the developments of my complicated life, and the factor of this *other* friend I have there. You claim I had introduced some element of sabotage concerning this girl – the mere specter of that relationship having frightened me to such an extent. In the end, I know you side with her, but you forgive me nonetheless. That's what I like about you, your uncompromising opinion on the affairs of the heart is only second to your gratuitous understanding of the shortcomings of, well, yours truly.

I hope you enjoy your travels during the holidays. If I don't speak to you before your departure, I will surely call you upon your return.

St. Louis

Washington, D.C.,

We are born free, but everywhere we are in chains. Rousseau had observed this truth which was to be immediately succeeded by a truism. Forgive me for this repetition of the obvious. I am simply responding to your papers.

You begin by saying that we as individuals have obligated ourselves in a social contract of natural liberties. Our multitudes have gathered and in this united entity, no one can assail any of its members without offending the body, nor can the body be victim without the members feeling the effect. Such is the theory of a social contract among a united people.

Yet in America, we persist in becoming assailed at the expense of certain underprivileged groups.

It is often ignored that the political order of democracy is fueled by its economic structure. I am concerned about your enthusiasm toward what is effectively called democracy in America.

You acknowledge at least that to sanction the right of occupancy on any piece of land outside of titles, it must be through labor and cultivation, not by vain ceremony. Rousseau had asked, when Vasco Núñez de Balboa, standing on the shore, proclaimed possession of the South Seas and all of South America in the name of the crown of Castille, was that enough to dispossess all of the inhabitants? I will answer yes, it is enough – enough insofar as it has been, and still is, a social and historical fact.

Not many years before Balboa, Columbus himself, with no less audacity, set off that same wheel of conquest and colonization. Imperialism.

American Democracy has evolved into a terrible beauty, a Kafkaesque sublime, a gateway intended for us but closed by our own volition. I do not contest the right of the majority rule. I simply appeal from the sovereignty of the people to the sovereignty of humanity.

The system has so efficiently mechanized all of its shortcomings that the cycles of inequity have become the terrible engines of this democracy upon which a force was found so powerful as to be not unlike a perfect monarchy. Mechanisms to foster apathy among the people, while preserving a vague notion that they had a choice in this matter, are constantly in motion. And the media, succumbing to the most base desires of the public, delivers what will sell, not what is sound. This miserable semblance of self and political affirmation distorts the true process of self-government.

With stratifications of wealth and poverty and a quota of welfare and unemployment, the upward/downward mobility becomes the apparatus of this economic structure. Balancing a careful form of wrongness by the right measure, this prowess acclaims its essence in its inequity. This we call opportunity.

Between the glass ceiling and the trap door, and the many closets for the socially deviant, this architecture of dissolution has its archways engraved with the old dictum, Give unto Caesar. But what is Caesar's?

Perhaps you believe I have relinquished my right to speak on this matter, having pronounced myself an ex-patriot. Still, it is about human decency. Let us not forget our origins. Our history is too short for such omission.

Paris

Miami,

So lovely to speak with you. You still hold that curious charm over me. Something in your voice, your choice of words…I don't think you realize what it does to me. One hopes you would not be so cruel as to continue otherwise. But I suppose this is my problem. And since you ask, no, I am not currently sleeping with anyone. (I am not sure I was supposed to answer that question.)

It was a few years back when we were writing each other more regularly. I reminisce. Sometimes we get caught up in life's many affairs and somehow get distracted. I would like for us to try again, our little exchange. I still think of you from time to time, despite the distance – or maybe because of the distance.

You will be hearing from me.

New Orleans

Sydney,

> You can watch water
> touch land by your feet,
>
> Your hands. You can see
> the blue of the sky-
>
> Sea's magnificence.
> You can paint driftwood
>
> This color mixing
> glitter and sand. You
>
> Will make the island
> more beautiful with
>
> Your presence. I will
> be thinking of you.

I am writing you in the heart of another winter. You on the other hand are presumably lodging your feet into pink sands, warm in the presence of a greater force – that island landscape with all its offerings of wind and wave. You are alive in the blue of the sea and sky, cobalt, electric.

Now, where was I? Yes, I was writing you this letter, a letter I would not send but give to you upon your return. – *Here*. I have missed you, I confess. But I recall you having permitted me to do so. Alas, I have.

I have been longing to see you again, your eyes, your face, always beautiful, rich with stories.

Toronto

Florence,

So, you have gone away. I hope it wasn't something I said.
Far be it for me to convince you otherwise. You might, however,
volunteer details as to what sort of wonderful has taken you away
from here – a job? School? Family, or friends?

It occurs to me the inchoate nature of our acquaintance – perhaps
more imaginary than real. But isn't this a part of being human?
You will allow me these words as a parting gesture.

There was so much I wanted to ask you. It seems silly, how
one's life is taken by the simplest things. A small exchange,
a friendly smile, someone who calls you by your name.
Sometimes it is enough to have these things to look forward to.

By now you must be settling in. We have diverted paths and
already I see myself doing a backward gaze at a woman whom
I wanted to know, but missed the chance. (Did I ever have a
chance?) I hope you don't mind. We come from different places.
Probably, we shall continue on our different ways. You have left
this place and I, somehow, will miss you – miss you in a way
I am not prepared to fully disclose.

I hope you find what you are looking for. Perhaps we shall meet
at a later time.

Paris

Providence,

The newest edition of the manuscript is herewith.

I was given the impression that there may have been some confusion concerning my reclaiming the older one which I had previously offered to you. I did not think it out of the ordinary that I should repossess this former copy. I was undoubtedly acting under the spirit of offering you a more current one. Beyond that, my taking back the older version was of no importance – and certainly of no political intent. Furthermore, I make it a general practice to eliminate outdated editions which seem to travel about. The purpose of this letter is to state this plainly.

It is true that of late, we have had our disagreements. And, as always, I understand that we will resolve them in due time. I have accepted this as granted, yes. The fact of our not understanding each other and my repossessing the manuscript are independent realities and any correlation between the two would require a great leap. I certainly was not acting in these terms; I trust you would not think that I would.

If you have any doubt, now or in the future, I should hope that you would feel comfortable enough to make it known to me directly, as I have always been, and will continue to be, forthcoming. If I have failed to demonstrate this, then an apology is in order. I apologize. My interest in our relation has always been benign. I sometimes feel the need to remind you that you were the one who needed the time and space to think things over. I had thought I granted you all that you had asked.

I hope this letter clarifies any misunderstanding. In any case, I appreciate you listening. I hope that we can relate to one another in a more positive context.

New York

Paris,

Home for the summer and already planning tours through Europe – you, woman of the world. I would expect nothing less. The Hotel Metropole serves a lovely continental. Let's meet on your next passage and we can rub elbows with all the U.N. people.

So this is what it has come to, our little correspondence. I can think nice thoughts with you over there. Something about writing each other, sending small things – private, like imaginary friends of childhood dreams. Once-removed, I find myself without defense. I like your letters. You should know that I do not take them for granted. I think they make me happy. It may be that I have learned more about you in these few instances than I had from being acquainted with you for those years prior. As for my letters, I hope you don't find the typed form impersonal. You would scarcely find my handwriting legible.

I was glad to hear you had found a new love – of poetry, no less. I believe such things can enrich one's life immeasurably. I have come across a rare manuscript which may interest you. I will send it out to you shortly.

Until then,

Brussels

Stockholm,

This makes several times I have tried to formulate this letter. It is difficult, especially after the way we had left each other. I am not finding the words. I don't even know if you are wanting to hear from me. I feel nonetheless obliged to express myself this time. Too often I declined to speak and was unable to defend myself.

It is true, I had wanted so much for this. But now, I wonder if it is even possible. I had believed we could have created something between us – we, who had spent our lives alone. The truly tragic part of this story is that we are incapable of giving to one another. So I come to realize, I have been completely mistaken.

And yes, somewhere, I was upset without wanting to show it, without wanting to recognize it. Now, I am taken by a kind of sadness and anger. I ask myself, what had I done? I feel so inadequate. So incapable. Yes, I am traversed. I am sorry.
We made the decision to not see each other as before. Remain friends, we had said. I doubt that this could be with all the unspokenness which surrounds us. In the end, I am not capable of continuing in this fashion.

I have taken on the poem again – the one thing I know how to do. This means I will no longer be responsible for whatever may be. A sorry excuse, I know. But in the end, I no longer feel any connection with this world, whatever.

I never thought I would write you these words. And still I am with difficulty. I wanted to clarify this before my departure (even post it from the airport) thinking I would return here and not have the courage. We turn the page – an act for which you were waiting, an act you were wanting to make. There it is. I waited a little and now it is done. You were right. We were hurting each other. Now we stop.

I will not close by saying I will speak to you soon, for we both know that this may not be so. I do honestly hope that you are better. Take care.

Paris

Prague,

Sometimes I forget the pathos in the poetry, which claims to reflect a certain pathos in my own life. And so I have developed a certain pang inside of myself designated for you. I somehow feel connected to you in this way.

And it is in the sweetness of your reception that I find myself sending you such words. I will surely run out of them before too long, but the kindness of your reply will linger on.

Place a stone on Kafka's grave for me.

Saint Paul

Dublin,

It was nice to see you during your passage. Moreover, your friends were all quite lovely. I was delighted to make their acquaintance.

If I was incapable of showing my appreciation, then surely it was criminal on my part. I believe I was undergoing something exceptional. I do hope I did not frighten you with that story of my violent emotional state. I should never wish to fall from your grace (if indeed I have procured such a place thereabouts).

Should you ever find yourself traveling through again, I would like the opportunity to host your visit, this time more properly.

London

Geneva,

Thank you dearly for your kind invitation to spend Christmas eve at your place. An exceptional offer – one that should not have fallen unaccepted.

I don't know what came over me, but I was suddenly seized with a desire to do nothing, alone. – Work on the poem (which I did, a little). – Re-write things I had been towing for months....

I continue my life of saying no to all that is good, concerning myself with all that is meaningless.

It seems only natural that I would feel a sharpened sense of solitude during this period where others assume the rites of being together, among others. What is it about these occasions which preclude such motions? The depression I feel during this season seems far too banal to recount. I shall not tire you with the details.

There you have it. I spent Christmas eve writing you these words. And so, in the end, achieved at least in part, I was with you in spirit.

With much love, Merry Christmas.

Paris

Boston,

Straight to the heart like a knife, with a twist, your salutations are. Enclosed herewith is a foreign cigarette package for your mixed media collage.

My last letter to you was during what was quite possibly the most chaotic time in my recent history. I have now settled into my new place. It is nice. It is nice to be home again.

Your invitation to visit stands, you insist. I think the chances of seeing you in Hartford may be higher. Neutral ground. Not that I would not want to see you in Boston, or elsewhere (you cannot be so innocent as you would like for me to believe). My desire to see you is greater than I can rationalize. That is why I cannot extend the same invitation to you. I trust you know I would always receive you regardless, and furthermore, on your terms.

You say you are finding yourself alone these days. Do you think alone you will stay?

There is no urgency in cherishing your solitude. Solitude will stay as long as it is welcome, sometimes longer. I have learned this all too well for myself. It is like that last guest at the party, intoxicated. You want to send them away, but instead, you take their car keys so they won't drive, and you are not the type to call for a cab.

I like this idea of this correspondence with you. It keeps me sufficiently preoccupied without the related dangers, and anticipation seems always once removed. I would like to hear from you again.

New York

Istanbul,

Forgive me for this brief façade of a letter.

My life here in all its outer appearance is stable, perhaps now more than ever. For better or worse, I am still trying to make sense of it.

There has been a kind of unease with which I have been leading my days, days which seem composed of a particular lack more than anything else.

Even as I become more responsible in an effort to save myself from an inevitable breakdown, I am strangely nostalgic of that period of unaccountability.

If only I could eradicate the desperate element from that other life, I would surely choose it again – though I should learn to be wiser in what I wish.

I know it is only a matter of time before I will find myself in that state. I can never be sure. Everything is precarious.

And though the job continues to be good to me, the knowledge of this good has not been a positive force in my present condition. I must convince myself every day that this is what I need.

This sounds very much like the language of recovery. What is good, or healthy, has not the same seductive element as what is despairing. This, above all constitutes the tragic part of my life.

I send you this letter despite its incoherent nature so as to not further delay my response. I fear this is all I can do at this time.

Paris

Iowa City,

I have received the parcel with your book, thank you. And yes, I have read it.

I should rightfully congratulate you on this recent publication. Also, I am flattered that you would request my thoughts on the matter. However, I wonder whether I am truly the one whose response you seek. My feelings have not really changed since you presented your manuscript in its earlier form. The important thing seems to be how you feel about it. Beyond that, my comments will surely be inadequate.

Your hard work has come to fruition with this event. I recognize this in its pure context. That is to say, I shall not conjecture beyond it. Nonetheless, I cannot help but think your work was a product of the MFA program and the numerous workshops which were to become the essential cultivating force for your book – you having rendered yourself to its many practices and having become a vital satellite in the vast network which is itself an institution.

This publication was the inevitable benefit of that career track you had secured for yourself. I, on the other hand, have long since contented myself with the notion that my work shall never see its day of print. I have positioned myself elsewhere. It is all too obvious the differences in our respective works, and the paths we have chosen for ourselves as concerns this business of writing. It is for this I would rather refrain from any critique. I had thought that you would acknowledge this.

I do regret having previously made the arrogant remark that even a dead animal could produce a book of poems out of those writing programs. I certainly did not mean it in that way. You are a writer by profession. There is no doubt that you are good at what you do. And you have the assurance of a brilliant career ahead of you. You have become an important player in an industry that propagates everything we know to be literary. I do not make light of it. Rather I am in constant awe of its power. I simply acknowledge that I have no part in that machine. Poetry cannot be conceived within this insular environment of fielding one's work in exchange for the works of others. In this closed circle, one will only succeed in achieving the attributes, never the essence.

My question to you is thus: Of what importance is my opinion? And yet, you insist. And to what end? Alas, if I were obliged to speak, I might say this: Treating your sexuality in your poems can be considered courageous by some – indeed, even your "mentor" suggests it in the preface. But what does he know of it? (Forgive me for this moment of indiscretion.) And, when did the incapacity of dealing with life's particular issues become the chosen thematic center of a literary endeavor? This reads therapy, not art. Finally, how did the written word degenerate into this? No. This is not the place. And this is not the exchange I would have sought. I would defer it once again. But, by the force of your insistence, you would have my opinion. Still, this would be of little consequence, for my words presume no gravity in your world.

Mariambad

Paris,

I was happy to hear from you. I see the perennial melancholy has us all close to its bosom.

As for your feeling uncertain of your present mode of existence, I hope that it is all right. This is what I have known for myself. Otherwise, I would have been in big trouble a long time ago, and in so many ways.

If you decide to come back to this city (and if I am still here), I would like to see you. You will let me know if I am undeserving of this.

Soon.

London

San Francisco,

My body has become estranged from itself since your departure. The bed, unforgiving as I turn and turn pawing at the mere vestige of your presence.

Boston

New York,

Yes it is true, I am the funniest man, here and elsewhere. I was glad I was able to make you laugh, if indeed I had succeeded in making you laugh. More laughter to follow.

I know I owe you some photos. But, alas, I did not bring my camera, and, more importantly, something in me is not allowing for the capturing of such images, though beautiful as the scenery may be. I suppose it could be nice to share them. There might even be some confirmation of my existence, however ephemeral.

Still, I fear nostalgia, like regret. I have tried to kill this part of myself in coming here. It could be that I have simply founded my citadel upon it, unwittingly. The irony still holds. After all, it has many layers, no? It was not long ago when I felt like a child. Now, I feel older than ever.

And though this city has been more precious than I could ever have imagined, still, it has had little affect on my feeling of slightness. And it is despite this perennial rapport that I have found the seeds of my loneliness and solitude, both. This thing proposes to make me stronger, if it does not succeed in erasing what little life force remains.

Did I ever think that I could really achieve this? – The poem, I mean. Yes, and as provisional, my breakdowns are in full bloom. It may not be long before I lose my composure in public. There would be no greater rebellion than this; there would not be a more perfect place than here.

What else can I say? Enough about me, how are you? I do hope that you are well. Your perseverance deserves admiration. Meanwhile, the rest of us are leading our little lives within the small prisons we have constructed in search of all that is ultimately fleeting.

In the end, there is probably good cause for my having stopped the madness. – The poem, I mean. I continue to remind myself, laughter is a good thing.

Take good care of yourself. I will talk to you soon.

Troyes

Saint Paul,

I am nearby in some broken down café with tea, cigarettes, thoughts of you....

Rather than calling and requesting your presence, or even making my general proximity known to you, I have opted to scribble this note to leave at your door. Possibly it is in fear of your answering machine, possibly in fear of your actual voice – I do not know of which. Doubtlessly a fear of some sort.

Snow outside, neon signs, conversations....

You are making plans for travel. Perhaps your mind is already in reconnaissance. Strange, this life. Sometimes we think of things without knowing exactly why. I guess I mean to say I am presently thinking of you. – You will forgive me. Yes, I have asked for this in the past. You have known this much about my nature.

I hope to hear from you, before you leave, or after you return – whatever is fitting. Perhaps you will think of me, perhaps not. It is outside my influence.

Minneapolis

Beijing,

I am writing you from a city half immersed in a dream, feigning forgotten.

Marco....

Carnivalesque and seductive. Intrigue hidden behind masks. Dances of death.

Marco....

The cleaning women wearing mystery in layers, dark as mascara. The gondoliers and their stories passed down with each pull and twist, thrust and turn.

Row after row. *Polo....*

All this turning water, and still the unquenchable thirst.

Venice

Paris,

The invitation stands for you to visit, now and whenever. I think that it would be to your benefit to spend some time away from the place which has now become associated with your affliction. Though I fully recognize what I have to offer will be short of any remedy for the particular malady you currently suffer, a simple change of climate could help initiate the arduous journey to recovery.

For my part, it may be that I continue to have feelings towards what we had shared. I shall not allow them to get in the way of your convalescence.

I shall feel comforted in your company. A friendship without complications, and without any misguidance. You be yourself, and I shall do the same. Seems a rare invitation in this world.

Let this be.

New York

Carpentras,

Thank you so much for the precious photos.

There is a certain quality in your images. I will not attempt to articulate my feelings towards them. Only, as I regard these pictures, I am taken to another place. Perhaps I mean that I feel present when I engage them, or when they engage me. Something which is not entirely evident in real life.

These comments are gratuitous, you realize. You know how I hate to speak of these things. But what am I really saying? You know this already. That's what's great about you. You understand me, despite my inability to express the most basic things.

In the end, I simply wanted to convey this: The world is a strange and wonderful place; whatever beauty exists, you will capture it.

Thank you, again.

Detroit

New York,

There may be no explanation. The dream state and all that is real are both at once elusive and inescapable. I lift the better part of my days into lightness. I want to share with you this life, this happiness. I brush off moonlight and mist from my eyes and find I am awake. Alive. And with you.

Thank you again for staying with me during your visit.
Your ethereal presence was like a beautiful dream in my semi-somnolent state. Still, my affection for you grows stronger in my waking. I suppose I knew from the start that you were lovely. I just didn't know to what extent.

I shall then await our next encounter.

Boston

Minneapolis,

Please excuse me. You will think this letter superfluous. Yes, I am writing from St. Paul, but this letter will contain no suggestion of any wish for you to be here. Granted, the words I write are infinitely more truthful than any speech that has proceeded from my lips. End of preamble.

You left abruptly that night we talked, left me in a state of sadness. Some relief too, of course, that we had finally spoken our minds, but sadness that it had to be. I only wish our talking put you at rest. You had anticipated such an exchange, only a matter of time. It had to be. And why not sooner? I, who have constantly returned your understanding, kindness, and purity with distance, indifference, impatience, irritability... I could go on.

Pain. I accept it. I accepted it from the outset when I took on the writing (or when the writing took me). But there was nothing in the contract, however, about others suffering in my cause. This I cannot bear. Doubtlessly you have been hardened. This is where our age difference is most visible. You are infinitely more experienced than I am in such affairs.

You must forgive me. You must, in effect, forget me. You came too close. You saw things you need not have seen, felt things you need not have felt. Many are my inadequacies. All of them, fear, inhibition, indecisiveness, breed upon themselves and I am left powerless. Until, at last, some instinct to survive compels me to act unjustly that I may feel detached. This had already happened once. And in fear of it happening again, I acted accordingly.

Often have I lied to myself. But never has any lie lasted long before I became thoroughly repulsed by it.

Maybe I am a fool to not be near you. You made me feel good. That is the truth. I am so sorry that I was unable to tell you that before. Please forgive me.

St. Paul

Milan,

Your letter fell into my hands in the midst of chaos. I am in the process of moving to another place, putting together another edition of the manuscript, and falling out of another relationship. I am breaking from all of this to reply.

It seemed your last letter was quite formal. Out of character, even. There is a certain spiritedness in you I admire. I couldn't help but notice the lack of it in your words. Also, there was no mention of *him*. I wonder if your life has taken a turn. Moving back home can sometimes be critical, in and of itself, I imagine.

I'm afraid you continue to occupy a certain part of me which I can only suggest. I suppose, in the end, I was surprised to receive your letter.

I have been thinking about the concept of the eternal return. I will be moving back into that apartment by the Picasso Museum where you had visited me two years ago. I still have that post-card you sent me, *The Young Harlequin.*

And with the anticipation of this move comes a feeling of solitude. This city has a way of inducing such anonymity. And the cooler weather has had its power to evoke memories of winter days.

Yes, I have thought of you.

You wondered whether I might be back in Milan. Forgive me for questioning your intentions. I have received such invitations before. You were not meaning to do that – inviting me. The wind no longer blows that way for me.

Paris

Tipasa,

Hartford is a dreadful city, redeemable only by the proximity of Boston, or New York – neither of the places which I have been decisive enough to go and see.

I had stepped out last night. And everything reaffirmed that I can no longer enjoy myself. I checked myself into a bar. It was hot and crowded and I could not stand the nausea. I thought of her, who had filled me with a vague notion that she might fly out to visit. I procured my own disappointment. I saw her eyes in one woman, her hair in another, until at last I could no longer picture her. I dashed out to the street and wandered around. How could I wish to return home when I knew what void awaited me there? Thoughts of Asia came to mind, or anywhere but here. Indeed, it is in the nature of such exile.

I have been having extreme difficulty with the most routine of motions: Sleeping (tossing, turning, nightmarish), eating (slowly losing appetite), smoking (less for pleasure, more for habit), drinking (I understand now the Welsh poet), writing (for it seems to go well with my smoking and drinking), reading (and with great resistance). I concede some recent notables: Italo Calvino's coy, *Invisible Cities,* vaporous like a dream; Milton, *Paradise Lost,* tight and useless – pure; Edmund Wilson, *To the Finland Station,* an unsuspecting novel, unsuspectingly melancholic; Hart Crane, *The Bridge,* this beautiful, beautiful failure – the most beautiful; Walter Benjamin, *The Arcades Project,* unfinished but not undone, sweet nostalgia; Elliot's *The Wasteland,* unrefreshing but still somehow innocent; and the cognate musings of Camus, *Exile and the Kingdom.*

Cities & Dust. Yes, I have been working on the poem. And the terrible result: Boredom & Effeteness. Derangement.

I am writing you from the all-night coffee shop, 4:30 in the morning. Surrounded by so many derelicts, and I feel myself deeply among them. I drew the line between the winners and the losers, not really aware of where I, myself, was standing. So it goes, and so it goes.

I think I need to hear from you.

Hartford

Rome,

I enclose herewith the abstract of the poem of which I spoke. I will be presenting this work at the gallery.

Admittedly, at no point during the twenty odd years of working on this text (even at my most undignified moment) had I ever envisioned this to be the finality of form. Still, I suppose, it needed to be, at least for the time. My one assurance, ironically, is the ephemeral nature of this beast.

It is true that my treatment of Faust is one devoid of any mysticism, and perhaps too, morality. It is one which renders Faust and Mephistopheles into a single being, divided. A conversation between the first brothers, the last. It is the testament of a stranger, made less strange in the telling. Existential in mood, granted. Nihilistic in tendency, perhaps. Post-structuralist in mentality...whatever that means.

I know that in the final count, whatever achievement I am able to claim will not pardon me from the atrocities committed against everything that is familiar. Still, I feel I had no choice. I regret. I only pray that one day I might be forgiven. Not because what I did was forgivable, but because I could not do otherwise.

Capua

Boston,

Thank you for the birthday note, and your musing on the new surroundings. I admit Boston seems a lifetime away, especially told to me, already twice removed. I sometimes forget that I grew up there.

Yes, I have moved to Paris. I am working again.

All in all, I must say that this city is everything it promises. Lights, the glitter in the Seine, and the sparkles on the Tour Eiffel (the sparkles are new), pedestrians everywhere, picnics along the Pont des Arts, brouhaha in cafés, brawling bistros, and the tiny cars which race the rond-points.

Then of course, couples kissing in the streets....

And I, well, I'll figure it all out one of these days.

I am thirty-three. I knew I would be one day. And, somewhere along the line, I told myself I would be elsewhere. So here I am.

This city is as lonely as I imagined.

Paris

Palestine,

Please excuse me. The fact of this letter is inordinate. And because I have no role in your affairs, this may come to you as an intrusion. What is to be done? It is in an effort to make right a wrong I may have caused. I shall make my words brief and to the point.

When I first arrived in late December, I recall you spending a great deal of time with our mutual friend. It was only with my continuing participation in your outings together that I had come to notice your vanishing interest in being present.

I am writing you now because, if it be the case what I have observed has some truth contained, I feel somewhat responsible. I must now properly recognize the cause of this negative outcome as linked to a situation which I had created – a situation real or perceived. I only wish whatever damage might be reversed.

And so it is, at the risk of being vain and presumptuous, I write to ask if it is in your faculty – indeed, if it be in your interest – to take steps toward restoring whatever rapport you and he shared.

I say this with sufficient urgency. As far as I know, you are the only person with whom he communicated. He had even confided as such.

Though it is not in my nature to assume the figure of a diplomat in the interest of others – I, myself, being depraved in so many of my own affairs – this loss for him, however, is one which does not rest well with me, thinking that I may have somehow caused it, and knowing for certain that I should never have even entered this city. In a world full of hate, what is there to do but desire from the outside a love we cannot gain?

I did not imagine I would write you like this. It would be quite difficult for me to say for whom I am doing this. So easily does one deceive oneself. Still, it is possible I am completely mistaken. If this be so, then please ignore this and discard it in its entirety. But if, by chance, there is even a remote possibility of my having noted something true, then please, please receive this accordingly.

I am terminating my regrettable sojourn here. I leave this place and everything behind. I am not enclosing a return address so you should not feel a need to reply.

Leningrad

Racine,

For the past few days I have been wandering around the city, taking trains and buses that lead nowhere, walking the crowded streets, a bag slung heavy with intent which I never open, smoking cigarettes in front of cafés, too afraid to enter, going to job interviews for positions I shall never assume.

Writing and rewriting this letter.

I have become lost.

And it is with infinite disdain that I realize how destitute I have become. Never would have I thought it possible, the breadth of vanity which could preside in a life, and still be mistaken as honor.

I have gravely failed you. I have been neither the inspired and productive artist nor the successful and supportive friend; rather a lame man trapped somewhere in between, ceaselessly working but still falling short of arriving at any moral or financial stability, and someone who still pretends at being an artist grasping at what remains, now, only false dignity, reduced to a pettiness I am not proud to know. I have ensured the disappointment you now feel towards me.

What I would give right now to have the time and the wherewithal to sit and read a book of poems – the inability for which you tease me almost affectionately. I am so tired. I want to sleep. I wish I could close my eyes and lie down for a week and wake up a renewed man. Instead, I feel a stone wall building itself inside me. I truly do not know what will follow.

If ever I survive this night it will be of the grace of my innermost being, which is the very essence of fear.

Berlin

Babylon,

Once again my response comes late. Useless to reproach myself, it cannot be helped. The inadequate man has his patent inadequacies. If I have learned anything, I have learned this much.

So it is with profound sadness that I return here, a place I once thought I knew, kept dear for the retrieving, only to realize in coming back, I had known nothing, that I was not to learn anything beyond it.

No use in lamenting over these things which have no significance. The greater tragedy in all this is that we live in a world dislocated. We are all but unhappy. Alone or together, endless without redemption.

There are things I shall never understand. Sometimes I feel myself so sensitive, so delicate as to be completely deranged by the slightest things. It is at these times I realize once again that I am not suited for this life.

I have been deliberating on these words, questioning the appropriateness of sending them to you. As if I have been haunted by some specter of silence, even as I formulate this letter, I know I would do better in saying nothing at all. If I am compelled to speak, then I am not certain from where this compulsion comes.

I am writing this letter in a period of change, with a confused sense of hope and sadness. I have become more aware of my solitude. And whereas in the past I was unable to relate anything by way of substance, I address you at this time for fear that it may no longer be possible after.

Sometimes I wonder if it was good of me to offer you the poem. Often in our encounters I had felt naked, without defense, as if I had divulged some great secret for which I felt ashamed.

There was only one reason that I stayed around. Paris... Paris was a pretext. If I am thinking of a move, it is because of you. The intimation of this end was present, even from the uncertain outset.

I have destroyed so many things around me. I seem not to know anything else. I only hope I have not interrupted your life in any great way.

Please forgive me.

Avignon

Eden,

There are letters I have written in the past which I am still not prepared to send. Things are complicated. There are many things which I find difficult to communicate, made still more difficult by the current standing of things.

My presenting the manuscript would be a great step in my coming forward, but this, too, must wait its proper time. I am still unsure of many things.

Please excuse me. This is long overdue and it is with the most recent exchange that this occurs to me. I have been known to overlook the obvious. I have no justification for them. I simply offer an explanation.

Though I continue in this confused strain, still, if only to clarify that one may better understand. It may be because of the recent fall, but I am suddenly overcome with a wish for you to see.

You are aware, the greatest fear an artist can have is the fear of being misunderstood. True, it is vain, but you will allow it, at least for the course of this letter. It may be that the one saving grace of this regrettable moment is that it furnishes me the pretext to do this much – which, in any other setting, would seem inappropriate.

In the face of impossibility, we move beside ourselves. Eloquence becomes crude, gestures of friendship become misguided. Too often we act out of fear, and the layers of pretense take over, where deep inside, we are simply in pain.

I do not hope to find absolution through these words.
On the contrary, it is quite possible that you will think less
of me after. But it has come to this and I must have you know.
You deserve much more than anything of this sort. And in this
feeling of inadequacy, I simply hope that you allow this letter
to deliver its words.

As I close out these thoughts, I see that it is getting light outside.
And soon I shall step out to greet the day. Coffee, the morning
paper.... So this is what this poet does at night – the aftermath to
which you had already been exposed on numerous occasions.

I had sworn to myself I would not be here. The time has come.
Elsewhere you will find me.

Exile

ABOUT THE AUTHOR

In 1986, at the age of sixteen, Hong would scribe the following verses which would later evolve into a struggle of two decades.

> *And did I know it then, that years later*
> *I would trace again and anticipate*
> *With tears which could not form at first, but would,*
> *Through affections derived of seasons*
> *And the grand gestures of the open sky,*
> *All the weighed wishes of the twilight moon,*
> *The windowpanes rain streaked with memories*
> *So murmurously dark with my desire?*

Beyond the fulfillment of these prophetic lines, the primacy of this poem would take command of Hong's existence. He would soon put aside his paintings and start on the path of this singular and near impossible task. Twenty years later, his epic poem celebrates this publishing event.